HALDHAR NAG

Selected poems

Translated by
Surendra Nath

BLACK EAGLE BOOKS
2020

BLACK EAGLE BOOKS

USA address:
7464 Wisdom Lane
Dublin, OH 43016

India address:
E/312, Trident Galaxy, Kalinga Nagar,
Bhubaneswar-751003, Odisha, India

E-mail: info@blackeaglebooks.org
Website: www.blackeaglebooks.org

First International Edition Published by
BLACK EAGLE BOOKS, 2020

Haldhar Nag
SELECTED POEMS
Translated by **Surendra Nath**

Original Copyright © **Haldhar Nag**
Translation Copyright © **Surendra Nath**

All rights reserved. No part of this publication may be reproduced, stored in a retrieval system, or transmitted, in any form or by any means, electronic, mechanical, photocopying, recording or otherwise without the prior permission of the publisher.

Cover & Interior Design: Ezy's Publication

ISBN- 978-1-64560-026-8 (Paperback)

Printed in United States of America

Preface

If we are going to admire Padma Shri Haldhar Nag as a man of little formal education who rose to fame on the literary scene in the country, we are going to miss the forest for the tree. It will also be an affront to his literary genius if we merely pity his background. It is neither despite nor because of the lack of education that the man rose to his present stature. He was always a giant in his mind, even when he lived in obscurity. He never noticed any dearth in his material world. In his early days of fame, when a television interviewer asked him how he coped with poverty, he replied: trees in the garden need watering and care, but trees in the forest grow by themselves. When the interviewer persisted by asking what the saddest part of his life was, Nag replied the loss of the famous poem *Suhudra Haran* (*The Abduction of Subhadra*) pains him exceedingly. It was a long poem in the form of a dance-drama (*geetinatya*), which came down for decades in the oral tradition. A single play of *Suhudra Haran* lasted nearly four hours. Never a script was recorded, but the performers knew it by heart. With the loss of the open stage dance-drama culture, this traditional poem has gone out of memory.

Haldhar Nag, who can recall some parts of the poem, is making efforts to retrieve the masterpiece from the memory of old-timers.

To him reviving his native language, Sambalpuri-Kosali, means the whole world. This he does by writing poems prolifically. Besides, he is forever on a crusade to save the dialect that appears to be on the verge of extinction. He misses not a single opportunity, when he meets the higher-powers in the government, to demand a Sambalpuri-Kosali Research Center in his native place. In fact, he has managed to get the proposal for a research center approved, though the construction is yet to start. It is his dream project where he wishes litterateurs to assemble and restore old manuscripts, set to paper the many tales about his land that are now surviving by word of mouth. It is also his dream to muster the services of translators to translate the priceless literary works in Sambalpuri-Kosali to other languages and even the classics of other languages to the native tongue.

So much about the man; it is time to speak about his works. I think Haldhar Nag deserves to be studied in greater depth, considering the volume and quality of works he has produced. My guess is, he may have written over 500 poems, but neither he nor anyone else has kept a count of those. Many of his manuscripts are lying unpublished in some sacks and satchels in his little house. And he is still at it, scribbling verses long and short. According to him, he writes (or dictates) the final version straight out. He does all the rough work in his head and not on paper.

His poems display a tremendous variation in length. They could be as short as a single stanza like *Paanch Amrut* (*Five Nectars of Immortality*) and as long as 1340 stanzas like *Prem Paechaan* (*Manifestation of Love*). He is at his poetic best in the long ones, the notable ones being *Mahasati*

Urmila (*The Great Sati Urmila*), *Achhia* (*Untouchable*), *Bachhar* (*The Year*), and *Sundar Sai* (*Surendra Sai*) among others. This book is a collection of short poems (short by Nag's standards). Nonetheless, I have felt tempted to add a few interesting episodes from a couple of long poems.

While many a present-day writer has focused on the trending theme of mythology by adding their imaginative twists to the storyline, perhaps, none has been as creative and original as Haldhar Nag in portraying mythological subjects. Take, for instance, Urmila; she has been highlighted as the neglected character of Ramayana by many writers in different Indian languages. Nag portrays her as a character neglected by authors and poets rather than by the plot of Ramayana. For originality, characterization, and descriptions *Mahasati Urmila* (*The Great Sati Urmila*) has remained his most popular poem. Read an episode from this poem in this collection to find an unexpected revelation. Nag, in his retellings, has taken up maligned characters and revealed them in glorious light. According to him, Kaikeyi is not the villainess that the world makes her out to be, but a farsighted woman who got Rama into exile to protect him from an imminent doom that haunted the throne of Ayodhya and took the blame of selfishness upon herself. About this poem, Shri Manoj Das, the author decorated with Padma Bhushan says:

"The source of inspiration that glorifies Kaikeyi in the poetry of Shri Nag is undoubtedly a sign of compassion built up over times, may be in the subconscious hearts of multitudes for centuries. It does not contradict the factual elements in the original, but expresses only a human and sentimental pity for a character that had been cursed for centuries. The poet's flow is irresistible and the metaphors he uses reveal a picturesque imaginativeness."

In similar vein, Pootana is not the demoness as the general perception goes but a devout and lovelorn mother, who by breastfeeding the Lord, merges into Him.

It is evident that Haldhar Nag primarily focuses on mythology, yet the diverse themes chosen by him cannot be overlooked. Social, historical, fabular, biographic, satire, patriotic, nature, comedy, and moralistic are among his array of subjects.

If there is one poet a majority of whose works can be rendered into symphonies, I would say it is Haldhar Nag. Such is the rhyme, rhythm, meter, beat, and scale in his lyrics, especially in the long poems. I admit, in translating poetry, much of the musical attribute is lost. That, unfortunately, is the limitation of translation. Those who can read the original in Sambalpuri-Kosali can easily see what I mean. For the other readers, I would refer them to the Internet to locate Haldhar Nag reciting his poems and discover for themselves the melody. This is another feather in the poet's cap. He is a bard and minstrel of the yesteryears. Even if one cannot understand the language, they cannot but notice the tempo of his rendition.

I have often wondered if Haldhar Nag graduated from a poetry school. Of course, that cannot be true, but my feeling arises from the abundance of figures of speech that appear in his poetry. Unknown to him, he sprinkles liberally the effects of alliteration, metaphors, internal rhyming, personification, onomatopoeia, and what have you in his usage. *Ghensali* (*River Ghensali*) is personification at its best, where the poet personifies a river in spate as a young lass in exuberance. And yes, he has come out with sonnets too. Read *Ati* (*Too Much*) to get a taste of Haldhar sonnet. The stanzas are spaced in 4, 4, 4, 2 lines, with a proper rhyme scheme. It leaves me in wonderment again

– If he did not go to a poetry school, then did God plant all these literary usages in his head?

For the sound effect, listen to *Chaetar Sakaal* (*The Morning of March*) – twelve stanzas replete with onomatopoeic works. Pity the translator who has to preserve the special effect in another language. I take recourse to the limitations of translation once again and state the obvious: Translations can never attain the beauty of the original. If we liken the original to an attractive painting, at best, the translation can be a replica or a photograph.

A hallmark of Haldhar Nag's poetry is what I call the Haldhar twist. It is particularly prominent in his short poems. The poet takes an abrupt turn in the direction in the last stanza, not necessarily for summarizing or moralizing. The surprise turn in the final stanza, instead, leaves the readers with a 'wow' effect. Very many poems in this collection display the Haldhar twist – *Our village Cremation Ground*, *A Cubit Taller*, *The Dove is my Teacher*, and *Old Banyan Tree*, to name a few.

If the translator is faithful to the words, the verses turn prose-like, and if he tries to keep to the rhyme and rhythm, much of meaning is compromised, what with colloquialism and regional proverbs. Yevgeny Yevtushenko has put across this dilemma with some jest: Translation is like a woman. If it is beautiful, it is not faithful. If it is faithful, it is most certainly not beautiful.

Now I ask myself if my translation is beautiful or faithful. There are 60 poems in here. I would like to believe, quite many of them are beautiful. But I leave it to the judgement of the reader.

Surendra Nath

Contents

Five Nectars of Immortality	13
Old Banyan Tree	14
A Cubit Taller	16
Wine	21
Lies Lead to Hell	22
River Ghensali	23
The Great Sati Urmila	25
Slumber	34
For a Little Broth of Rice	36
The Cuckoo	39
Market of Illusion	41
The Dove is My Teacher	43
Our Village Cremation Ground	48
Mother Pootana	50
Juapuni	58
Regard for Soil	61
Bulbul	63
Animals and Humans	65
What Do We Do	66
What Else Could Have Happened	68
Lantern	70
Fire	71
Too Much	72
Profit	73
Kamdhenu	74
Greatness	75
The Jealous Always Suffer	77

Make No Silly Excuses	78
Summer	80
Rains	81
The Harlot of Tikarpada	82
Danseuse	83
Demon	85
On the Death of Budhadev Das Cries Mother Samlei	87
Kunjel Para	88
First Clean Yourself	91
The Younger Brother's Courage	93
Why Did He Leave His Home	95
Warning	98
Swachh Bharat	100
Mahua Tree	102
Butterfly	103
Neem Tree	104
Smeared with Colours, The Old Man was Cremated	105
Radhe-Krishna	107
The Matter Ends Here	125
The Minister and the Beggar	127
God Kalia of Priest Luru	129
Bhai Jiuntia	133
Spring Tune	135
The Morning of March	137
A Song in Sanchar Tune	139
The Soul is Real	140
The Slaying of Kalapahad	145
Conscience	152
Just Think of It	154
A Letter to Poet Haldhar	155
Light of the Earthen Lamp	157
Chhanda Charan Avtar	158
The Village Chowkidar	160
The Poet	162
The Translator	164

Five Nectars of Immortality

Let the nectar always flow
From the seven seas
From the moon in the skies
From mother's breast
From noble principles
And from the poet's scribbles

Old Banyan Tree

Generations have gone by
And it stands with its head high
The old banyan tree of the village
To the left of the entrance path

Its canopy vast and widespread
As wide as a threshing ground
The branches extend far out
And like ropes its roots hang down

Great grandfathers and their fathers
And friends and people known
Used to climb the tree and swing
On its roots when they were young

Mynah, *haral** and other birds
Flock to it when fruits get ripe
From morn till eve, people sit under
Chatting noisily with much hype

In the month of May at midday
When the roads are blistering hot
Under this tree, travellers rest
Then they go on after their halt

The groom comes to take his bride
From here they start their procession
The bride departs from under here
The wedding comes to conclusion

Here they bring the dead and place it on the bier
Anoint it with turmeric and gooseberry
Women return home from this spot
Leaving behind the ritual pottery

As night advances thieves make entry
From village homes they steal
Under this tree they distribute
Their loot - money gold and utensil(s)

The lover waits for his lass
In the twilight of dawn
They promise to elope
Under this tree of banyan

It sees, it knows, it hears, it finds
But it speaks not a word
It stands like a mute witness
With its strong arms spread outward

---

* *haral* – a type of bird

A Cubit Taller

In a hillside cave sat meditating,
A saint, he was a great soul.
Single-mindedly he was praying,
Since a time no one could recall.

Over his limbs swarmed termites,
Enclosed he got in a termite mound.
On that mound sat a bird;
Not far a hunter was on the round.

He took aim and shot an arrow,
Stricken the bird came down rolling.
The saint's face was splattered with blood,
As the bird lay, its wings beating.

Writhing, struggling and chirping,
The bird finally went still.
Disturbed was his meditation,
The saint saw a bird killed.

Like the banana leaf he shook,
And shivered out of anger.
Said he, "Who caused before me,
Such an act of blunder?"

With folded hands pleaded the hunter,
"Sinned I have, unknowingly.
Saint's meditation I disturbed;
Do pardon me my folly."

Said the saint, "For your sin,
Penalty your due, you shall pay.
The fruits of my penance,
You have frittered them away,"

Said the hunter, "I shall recompense,
All fruits I shall pick for you now.
How much fruits do you desire?
O great saint, let me know."

Said the saint, "You sinner hunter,
This fruit is given by the One.
His name is Govind Gopal*
To the faithful He is well-known."

The hunter said, "Govind Gopal!
I shall bring him to this place.
All fruits I shall have him give you,
Please wait here for some days."

"Govind Gopal, Govind Gopal,"
Calling he roamed ceaselessly.

Day and night, without care for hunger,
He searched the woods sleeplessly.

Calling aloud at sundown,
In the forest he was roaming.
When someone hailed, "Govind Gopal
Is here presently waiting."

As if he got back his life,
In such haste he did run.
Into a cavern on a hill,
In the dusk he was shown.

Inside the cave burned firewood,
Hacked hands were piled in a corner.
Many people had been drawn in,
And beheaded at the altar.

An evil priest stood casting spells,
Goddess Kali he prayed.
He kept an axe a yard in length,
Razor sharp was its blade.

He pushed the hunter's neck within
The slaughter posts and a blocking beam.
He mocked, "Watch now, Govind Gopal
Will come and you can catch him."

"O Kali, eat this sacrifice,"
Said the priest and raised his axe.
Suddenly came a thunderbolt,
With showers and lightning streaks.

The axe to one side was thrown;
The evil priest was unconscious laid.
Broke the knots of sacrificial posts,
The hunter stood up unscathed.

Goddess Kali's image he glimpsed,
One part with her hair let down;
Another part was a boy with a flute,
And peacock feather on his crown.

When he called, He responded,
The One who played the flute.
The hunter grabbed Him by the arm;
"Hey you boy," he called out.

"Looking for you I am tired,
And you are hiding here!
Don't delay now, let's go quick,
The saint must be waiting there."

Forcibly he dragged him straight,
And took him to face the saint.
"O saint, I've got Govind Gopal,"
He said, "With you to acquaint."

Astounded at seeing the Lord,
The saint fell prostrate at His feet.
Perplexed and confused within,
He joined his hands to entreat.

"Whole life I have been praying,
You obliged me not even once.

At the call of a mere hunter,
How did you turn up at once?"

Said the Lord, "For thy own benefit,
You've been calling me for favour.
For else's help the hunter called;
He stands a cubit taller."

---

* *Govind Gopal – A different name for Lord Krishna*

Wine

Drink on, O drink the whole world,
Drink away to your heart's content.
Drink all that you may,
Wines in the stock are sufficient.

That wine will sway you,
Your mind will be joyous and merry.
Intoxicated, you'll forget,
The world's bondages illusory.

Entire life you'll be intoxicated,
Once you've tasted that wine.
The more you drink of it,
The more the flavour gets fine.

That wine is elixir of Ram,
That is stamped in the scriptures.
It has no price, no colour,
No bottle or peg measures.

Great men have given us free,
Pots of that heady nectar.
What you drink in the name of wine,
Is venom of the *gokhar**.

---

* *gokhar* – a type of poisonous snake (cobra)

Lies Lead to Hell

Telling lies, brings more treasure,
With treasure, comes more desire,
With desire, comes more indulgence,
With indulgence, come more diseases,
With diseases, comes the death knell,
With life gone, one lands in hell.

River Ghensali*

Listen O Ghensali, wait a while;
Where do you go rushing by?

Roaring, churning as if in anger,
You run down in Kali's figure.

Sleeping you had been peacefully,
In the Baisi Khalsa** valley.

Startled, you run in a single-minded
Across mounds, ditches, corners and bend

Forsaking joy and love of mother's house
Where will you enter as a live-in spouse?

You want to meet friends of yours,
Ang, Ib, Tel, Jira, Koel rivers^.

Your heart is excited and mind flitting,
Like a young girl to elope is waiting.

Bear in mind matters future and past.
Further you run, more you'll be slashed.

Let me say a word, listen Ghensali,
One trait of yours with mine does tally.

Over low and highlands you cross,
I too surmount my joys and sorrows.

You are heading to the deep seas,
I too am heading to rest in peace.

■

---

* *Ghensali – A river that originates from a spot close to village Ghens – the poet's village.*
** *Baisi Khalsa – a pair of hills between which the river commences/ originates*
^ *Ang, Ib, Tel, Jira, Koel – Names of rivers of the same network as Ghensali*

The Great Sati* Urmila
(An episode from the long poem of same name)

Ravan's daughter-in-law,
Sulochana was a lovely lady.
Fair was her complexion,
Like fire glowed her body.

Her face looked as though,
The full moon ascending;
Yogis would tear their matted hair,
Their minds would go raving.

Even on moon there are dark spots,
But on her face not a blemish;
The beauties in all three worlds,
She surpassed them with ease.

Over ages sat god and made her,
And made her so flawlessly;
Though born on mortal earth,
Her beauty was heavenly.

Shimmered her silken clothes,
Gold embroidery threaded;
On her breast sparkled necklaces,
With sapphires and diamonds studded.

Her steps so soft, an ant won't crush,
Anklets on her ankles did chime.
Her limbs were decked in finery,
One was sure to forget the time.

Like the black bee on *champa* flower,
Her topknot graced her hair.
The poet would fail to describe,
Sulochana's complete attire.

She was wife of Indrajeet,^
Like Parvati in chastity;
To break her bangles of *lac*,*
No one had such temerity.

No count there was of maids,
Those that were at her service;
If one were to evaluate her,
She would be the queen of paradise.

In a palanquin she lay swinging,
On a mattress soft and downy;
On a red silken pillow,
Her head she rested gently.

Suddenly a severed hand,
Landed in front of her;

'Has someone chopped it off,
And cast away in anger?'

Startled as if in a nightmare,
A scream she let out loud.
Young maids encircled her,
All dangers to keep out.

After a while, from the palanquin,
She alighted on the floor.
Seeing the severed hand,
Her head was sapped all the more.

She saw it right, identified,
It was her husband's hand;
Shape, colour, ring on the finger,
It was the right hand.

Yet her mind doubted somewhat,
She slid down and sat apart.
'If someone else's hand I touch,
My chastity would depart.'

Gifted she was, she took a chalk,
And dropped it on the hand.
Said she "Write quickly and truly,
Whether you are my husband."

And soon began the hand,
With the chalk to scribble,
"O Sati Sulochana today,
I fought a battle terrible.

"While fighting valiant Lakshman,
In fury struck me with arrow.
My head is lying at Ram's feet,
My hand lies before you.

"The body is on the battlefield;
Go there in haste dire,
Take all pieces, get a glimpse of Ram,
Then commit suttee[1] on my pyre.

"Release from world we shall achieve,
Upon seeing Ram's face, my dear;
This is your husband Meghnad,
Thus my script I end here."

On the other side on Subalaya Hill,
Ram was exchanging banter.
Exhausted, they were discussing,
About the day's encounter.

Said Ram, "Tell us Vibhishan,
You know everything.
Wherefrom is this craft,
Across the sky it comes flying.

"It is going not here and there,
But straight to us it is heading.
Voices of women are heard inside,
Some crying and some sobbing.

"Upon son Meghnad's death,
Has Ravan started to worry?

Has he come to return my Sita,
With kin and wife Mandodari?

"Or with eight dancers queen Sachi
Is making her appearance?
Or is it Yogin Mahamayi,
Or goddess Bhawani perchance?"

Vibhishan said, "Sulochana,
The Sati this is, Lord do watch.
Of her chastity, let alone humans,
Among gods there's no match."

Hearing Vibhishan laughed Hanuman,
With hand on his nose mocking:
"If demons' wives be called Sati,
Then in hell the best is cooking.

"With all efforts, would glass be gem,
And would brass turn into gold?
Champa fruit you term as guava,
You want us to be fooled?

"*Lepher* cannot become *Kanjer*[2] dish,
Nor can cat be a tiger small.
Can *kua babri*[3] be same as basil,
Or can crow caw the cuckoo's call?

"Indrajeet's wife is related to you,
Your brother's daughter-in-law,
That's why unto a demoness,
You name Sati without a flaw.

"Widowed, barren and unkempt head,
She's the reason her husband is dead.
You give a demoness Sati's title,
Have you no shame for such a deed?

"Prior Sati's death, her husband dies,
Have you heard of such ever?"
At the words of Hanuman,
Ram controlled his temper.

Insult of Sati and of saint,
Never in life had Ram endured.
Besides, Vibhishan had never
Talked matters loose and blundered.

But unto the devotee Hanuman,
He could say nothing stronger.
Ram bit his lip and suffered him,
And overcame his anger.

Shortly the flying craft came down,
Right before Ram it landed.
The very craft of Lanka's Ravan,
In which Sita was abducted.

Crying noisily a bevy of women,
From the craft did alight;
In the centre walked Sulochana,
Like full moon on a starry night.

If they stood in row, she would look,
A shiny pendant on jewellery.

In a column she would appear,
Like on banana cluster, a bell flowery.

Sulochana saw god Ram,
His winsome attractive figure;
Prostrated herself at his feet,
And bowed with respect and revere.

Full of devotion she kneeled,
And took the dust of his feet.
With folded hands she said, "O Lord,
I had been waiting for this treat.

"My sins of a hundred past lives,
Are absolved by Your sight.
I beg You to give me,
What my husband did write.

"Give me O Archer his head,
That I may hold and walk into fire;
Creator of world, O valiant Ram,
Do fulfil my final desire."

With both hands, held Ram,
Indrajeet's severed head.
Said he, "Take Sati Sulochana,
Keep in your palms tightly held."

Ram then spoke to Meghnad,
"Tell me this honestly.
Is Sulochana Sati or not?
Do reply immediately."

Upon Hearing Ram's query,
Eyelids opened and spoke the head,
"O Ram, Sati is Sulochana,
It's the truth that I have said."

Ram said, "Sati is Sulochana,
That's what you maintain.
Husband's death prior to Sati's,
The Vedas do not ordain.

"While Sati Sulochana is yet alive,
How could you depart this life?
Thus they doubt valiant Hanuman,
Angad, Nal and Jambvan."

Indrajeet's severed head said,
"O Archer Ram, do listen.
In all Yugas truth always won,
Never has it been beaten.

"You all witnessed today's battle,
We fought warrior against warrior.
Lakshman and I were not fighting,
Amid two Satis was the warfare.

"Though a Sati was Sulochana,
She lived in luxury royal.
In abstinence prayed Sati Urmila,
Sacrificing all things material."

So saying the head closed its eyes
But lips quivered in mumble:
"In war between Satis, won a Sati
That was the Great Sati Urmila"

---

^ Indrajeet –Son of Ravan, Meghnad was also called Indrajeet because he had defeated Lord Indra and conquered the heavens.
* lac – a material like sealing wax out of which bangles were made in the olden days
1. suttee – Ancient Indian custom of a widow immolating herself on the funeral pyre of her husband
2. Lepher, Kanjer – Lepher is an inedible leaf which looks like Kanjer. But the latter makes a tasty dish
3. kua babri – a type of plant whose leaves look like those of basil. The basil plant is used for worshipping and for medicinal purposes

Slumber

Sleepy drowsy, O Slumber,
Why do you come about?
My eyelids are getting droopy,
I am about to pass out.

For Goddess Saraswati to arrive,
I expectantly wait.
If you lull me to sleep,
Fish might escape from the net.

I beseech you, at such a time,
Near me don't appear.
Stroking me to a pleasant lull,
My life, do not destroy.

With your blessings are surviving,
Lifeforms fifty-six crore.
My share you break in two,
And one half you keep in store.

One part, give me when I'm tired,
And of you I start thinking.
In the morrow for a living,
I need to get working.

Pleasure of your lap is for the rich,
Who wear silken clothes.
Gluttony and waste of money,
Are in bad taste, I loathe.

The mind is never still,
Out of anxiety it flees.
Through wind and space, it flies,
Crossing over seven seas.

The lamp of life is turning dim,
The oil is burning down.
At this point, I'm struggling,
When the time is already gone.

If you wish for me deep sleep
Just for a while you wait.
I'll be lying in the cremation ground,
Spread out long and straight.

Blessed by Saraswati writes the poet
These lines are true forever.
"Of earth I am, unto earth I shall go,
My body insects will devour."

For a Little Broth of Rice

Mountains all around sky high,
This is the dam on Indravati,
Sited within a dense forest.
Water it holds like the ocean,
To the eye it is the fiercest.

College students on Dussehra vacation,
Went there on an excursion.
Roving here and there they saw
A shaky old woman breaking stones,
Beside a mountain hollow.

Shrivelled, wrinkled was her skin;
Her dark body sweated plenty,
She was aged eighty or ninety.
'Let's snap her picture,' said they,
And gathered round the woman.

With their cameras when they clicked,
The old woman was very piqued.
"Scoundrels, you be eaten by tiger,
"Want my photo, you gutter sleeper.
I am like your grandmother.

"Go that way, women workers,
Young ones you'll find galore.

Queue up there and get lewd.
A ripened leaf, ninety-year-old-
Woman's picture why you shoot?"

One of them asked, "Grandma tell,
At this age, so hard you toil.
Such back-breaking labour!
We are struck with wonder,
Profusely all of us swelter"

The old woman said, "Listen, Dear,
I used to dazzle in my year.
Daughter of a village head and a chief's bride,
Smart, showy and qualified,
Gorgeous-looking was I.

"At home we had riches abundant,
Hundred acres of farming land,
Pulses from the minor field,
Gunji, Mandia, Kudo,* peanuts,
Our house was always filled.

"There never was any dearth,
On me I wore lots of gold,
I lived in joy and plenty.
Servants and workers, at my call,
I was a lady of property.

"The zamindar was my husband,
Two young sons I had.
The sin of some life past,
In Indravati dam waters, blimey!
All were drowned and lost.

"I the accursed, gobbled all,
None ahead nor back to call.
Death, why you took me not?
For a little broth of rice,
At this age, I slog a lot."

Time is the strongest of all,
Like cart-beam rises and falls,
Fortunes turn, kings become beggars.
Here's landlady Dhira breaking stones,
For a little broth of rice.

■

---

* *Gunji, Mandia, Kudo* – *crops, cereals*

The Cuckoo

Cuckoo, you sing staying hidden,
Within the blossoms of the mango.
Your song drips like drops of honey,
One feels content hearing your coo.

Among birds you are the queen,
Like a black cat dark is your lustre.
Your voice is sweet like sugarcane,
Minds of folks with it you allure.

In the crow's nest you lay your eggs,
And from that spot you disappear.
Lonesome you roam the deep forests,
For kith and kin have no desire.

I hear it's written, when Krishna
Went to see *Dhanu Yatra,**
Mother Yashoda's wails of yearning,
As an onlooker you saw.

In folklore we hear, once a year,
On Return Car Festival day,
Like a newlywed bride you cry,
And go to your in-laws on tenth day.

That's when the lizard carries clothes,
And the bear carries the utensils;
*Runi*** bird anoints you with makeup,
*Chithei*** bird makes shrilling trills.

The woodpecker plays the drum, *Sargana***
the trumpet,
The dove becomes the doorkeeper,
The Mynah goes with band and sweets,
And clears the path as the mediator.

You are not seen, your melody is heard,
You talented and bashful bird;
The gifted ones are seldom seen,
But their worth spreads forward.

■

---

* *Dhanu Yatra*- Kamsa invites Krishna (when he was a boy) to a festival named Dhanu Yatra, with the intention of killing him. Krishna overcomes all obstacles posed by Kamsa and finally he (Krishna) kills him.
** *Runi, chithei, Sargana* – types of birds

Market of Illusion

Illusive market at Guava Groves,
Going and coming are people in droves.
Thugs and thieves, men and women,
About the marketplace all are keen.

How nicely the confectioner sits,
The toothy is selling peanut sweets,
Balls of rice in jaggery soaked,
Popped rice sweets rounded rolled.

Saris named *Kakan Payer, Baul Maal,**
And red free end of *Danti Gayel.*
Designed saris *Dus phoolia, Chandan Kura,*
Clothes he sells, Manu the weaver.

Green spinaches, *lehentia, nalita,*^
Radish, tomatoes and brinjal dried.
Beans, okra, drumsticks and arum,
Are displayed by the gardener woman.

To sell dishes, pans, bowls, pitchers,
Sits cross-legged, nephew of the brazier.
He weighs using the lever rod,
He calculates and takes his price.

The goldsmith sells earrings of gold,
Nose ring, tops, chains and studs.
Betel-shaped hairpins and bracelets,
Toe rings, armlets, and anklets.

Buying and selling at every instant,
Not a moment the market is vacant.
Crowded is the market of illusion,
Home they return, when money is gone.

∎

---

* *Kakan Payer, Baul Maal, Danti Gayel, Dus phoolia, Chandan Kura – types of saris*
^ *lehentia, nalita – types of leafy vegetables like spinach*

The Dove is My Teacher

A pair of doves male and female,
On a silk cotton tree did dwell,
In the forest, on a hill slope;
Displaced had been their home,
Due to mankind's greed to develop.

They loved each other every moment,
With affection their hearts were content.
Emotionally they were united;
Their minds were attached inseparably,
Not once were they separated.

Whatever the female dove said,
The male every word obeyed.
He never crossed the line;
He followed her like on a leash,
Listening to her all the time.

Many days passed this way,
She was in the family way.
To cradle her babies she longed;
As the time to deliver approached,
She was restless to get it over.

A pair of eggs she laid,
Afterwards no food she ate,
She sat on the eggs brooding,

Like a yogi sits in a posture,
Neither swaying nor moving.

Hatched the eggs on day twenty one,
Out came chicks with good concern.
The parents saw their chicks;
They picked tender foods for them,
And fed them into their beaks.

Hearing the soft tweets of their boys
The two birds had cause to rejoice.
They held them under their wings,
Afar from dear chicks never they went
They foraged nearby till evenings.

In time their little wings grew up,
The chicks were able to flap.
They played within their bough;
When they would grow some more,
Their parents they would follow.

But who knows of plans divined?
What's in store for whom destined?
One day the doves went foraging;
They told their chicks "Do not stray,
Do not climb down from the tree."

Looking for food they went faraway,
While searching there was much delay.
The chicks got very hungry;
Down they climbed the tree,
And in the shade they made merry.

Watched a hunter from a distance,
And thought, 'I will get a chunk,
Today a good meal I will afford.'
He salivated at the thought of,
Fried young game bird!

He laid straight a trap of net,
In it he scattered some grains as bait.
A little away he waited in hiding;
Their stomachs were growling with hunger
In came the chicks hopping.

To eat the grains they came rushing,
Got trapped and started struggling.
Piteously they looked for a way out,
Caught they were for their greed,
"Mother, Father," they called aloud.

The pair of doves at that instant,
Returned with food to their nest.
They called out, "Come dear ones,
What tasty food we have brought!
You'll relish eating these crumbs."

They saw the chicks from the nest missing,
And cried out, "Where are you O darlings.
Come running, come quick here."
Calling aloud their throats were parched,
Yet, the chicks did not appear.

Down they saw in the hunter's mesh,
The chicks were struggling in distress.
Their voice was already choking;

"Oh Mother, Oh Father," they were crying,
Their necks trapped in the net string.

The female dove fell down dazed,
She cried beating her chest and head.
"O my dear little children!
A nice home I had made,
It got washed in the torrent.

"Where will you go leaving me alone?
From my womb you were born.
You're leaving me childless;
Take with you this ill-fated mother,
Without you I'll be lifeless."

The chicks were crying in distress,
Mother dove could bear no longer.
Into the death-trap she dived;
Holding her sons in her wings,
On their beaks and cheeks she kissed.

Father dove cried perched aside,
"My love you also lurched inside.
All of you went leaving me alone;
My happy home is burnt to ashes,
We've been hit by *Yama*'s* baton.

"My love leaving me alone,
Where will you go with our sons?
Oh my dear companion;
With whom shall I romance,
In the forests and in mountains?

"Leaving me behind where are you headed?
For even a moment we never separated.
O my necklace, my beauty!
You feed me first and then you eat,
O my devoted *Sati***.

"My sons and wife you've split from me,
Letting me sit like a leafless tree.
It is all in my destiny;
Fie on my shameless life,
Life I cannot live lonely.

"Near and dear I have none.
Why must I go living on?"
So saying, he let out a blare;
Crying aloud he too dived,
Into the hunter's snare.

The hunter saw it all cheerfully,
And gathered his trap carefully.
All the doves he collected;
Shutting them in his cage,
Towards his home he headed.

Male and female doves are divine soul(s),
In the body called tree they dwell.
Illusion is the trap that's sprung;
Grain is greed and children attachment,
Hunter is the time of doom.

■

---

* *Yama – God of death*
** *Sati – a woman who is chaste and devoted to her husband*

Our Village Cremation Ground

In the evening jackals howl,
Also cackles of hyaenas abound,
This is our village cremation ground.

Around it is a mango orchard,
Therein owls and *jeen^* birds,
Sit and hoot aloud.
From tree to tree they flit around.
The other side below the shady banyan,
Lies the shrine of the deity.
This is our village cremation ground.

The deity jumps on branches of trees,
Ululates she at the top of her voice.
Soil and dust, she flings around,
Palm fronds make noisy sound.
Swing is swinging, fire is burning,
Like the bonfire mound.
This is our village cremation ground.

On new moon night, a witch grazes,
Holding a lamp on her chin.
Fully naked, hair spread open,
Grazes she riding *Bir Bahan**.

With legs up and sharp cane in her bite,
She goes trampling all around.
This is our village cremation ground.

A mother's ghost grunts to deliver,
Groans and warms her stillborn with fire.
Nails as long as the fingers span
She chases people to slash
Outside stands her elder brother
The ghost of a bachelor who died young.
This is our village cremation ground.

Those possessed and haunted by spirits,
Their curse is dispelled by the exorcist.
Blood, trickery and black magic found,
He despatches them to the burial ground.
With one black hen sacrificed,
Spirits and ghosts are satisfied.
This is our village cremation ground.

Cremation ground looks fearsome,
But this ground is our real home. / our home
To this ground have journeyed many,
Yet to travel are so many.
To this end we shall all journey,
At this place we shall all crowd. / finally crowd
This is our village cremation ground.

------

^ Jeen birds – *a type of bird that is believed to chirp aloud when someone is about to die*
* Bir Bahan – *An imaginary mount that witches are believed to be riding on*

Mother Pootana

(An episode from Manifestation of Love)

With a shock, awoke Kamsa,
Startled out of his stupor.
Like a cobra he hissed,
And yelled "I shall slaughter.

"From Devaki has been born,
Last night, Kamsa's enemy.
Like squishing a shrimp,
To death I shall strangle him."

Swaying up and down his sword,
He rushed towards the prison.
Hearing the baby's cries,
He life was filled with terror.

Teeth clenched and gnashing,
He dashed into the quarter.
Said, "Let me wipe out my foe;
Hand me the child, Sister."

Devaki said, "Brother Kamsa,
This is a girl, not a boy.
Killing a girl what fame will you earn?
The world upon you will fie."

Kamsa said, "Sister, don't fool me,
I know better than that.
Mahishasur was killed by Durga;
A girl was she not?

"Very clever all gods are, dear,
They've played a lot of frauds.
In Satya and Treta Yugas,
They've killed Asura hordes.

"Be it a girl or a boy,
My doom is your progeny.
If I let go now, danger lies ahead,
They'll play some trick on me."

He snatched the baby and ran,
Towards the rock called *Darpan*.
He raised the baby to kill it,
By crashing it on the stone.

With a giggle, Goddess of Lightning,
Flew high into the heavens.
In amazement looked around Kamsa
Searching in all directions.

With laughter spoke the Goddess,
"Hey you demon Kams,
Keep in mind, you'll be destroyed,
Along with your entire race.

"With your ego, you'll bite the dust,
Kamsa, you foolish monster.

The child who will kill you is growing up
At Nanda's house in Gopa-pur."
*
Wailing aloud frantically,
Pootana was running in frenzy.
Her body was half bare,
Her hair was loose and frowzy.

"From my chamber, Kamsa took away
My son, he hasn't yet come back.
A day is past and then the night,
But of him there is no track.

"Where did he go, whom he gave,
His son he took from me."
Every nook and corner
Of Mathura town she was combing.

She recalled from somewhere,
And ran towards the rock *Darpan*.
At that instant a *Gandharvi**
Was speaking from the heaven.

"Hey demon Kamsa, that child
Is growing at the Nanda's in Gopa."
Hearing this her heart burst out,
Stricken with panic was Pootana.

Holding Kamsa's feet, she cried,
"To whom you gave our son, tell?
Your own son you gave to someone!
How could you be so cruel?

"My breasts are aching,
Milk is oozing forth.
I'll go to Gopa and feed
My boy from my breasts both."

Hearing her occurred an idea,
The demon hatched a plan.
'Pootana will surely go to suckle,
She won't wait an instant.'

He said, "O Pootana, don't wipe
Your breasts full of milk.
The royal doctor's medicine I'll dab,
No longer will they ache.

"Go and feed our son,
And bring him back, if you can.
He'll be the prince of Mathura,
King and Queen, you and me."

He got some poison from somewhere,
And applied on her nipples both.
He said, "Pootana, go quickly,
To Gopa-pur sally forth."

Pootana was not scared at all,
That she might get murdered.
She was not ashamed or shy,
That she was half uncovered.

Pootana could see nothing,
The world seemed dark to her.

Her sight was fixed wholly
On her son, only her son.

How to reach Gopa-pur,
And breastfeed her child.
Like floodwater she rushed,
Restless was her mind.
*

Entire Gopa was agog with the news
That the queen had birthed a child.
So what if she was past the age?
Destiny was on her side.

First one son from Rohini,
Fate offered them in blessing.
The king got his Karma's due,
The child has been thriving.

To get a son they had pledged
Fasts and worships umpteen.
Pleased have been the gods and fulfilled
The desire of King and Queen.

Smiling with glee, all Gopa women,
In the king's palace were crowded.
Cutting the umbilical cord,
Washing and fomenting they completed.

In a nappy, they lay him in the swing,
And swung him spellbound.
Songs they sang with no restraint,
It seemed the swing would fall down.

At that time, frantic Pootana
Entered the king's manor.
Seeing her frightening figure,
Everyone fled out of fear.

Dishevelled her hair and clothes,
Uncovered was her breast.
To get a glimpse of her son,
Her mind was not at rest.

As she entered, she saw the child;
He was playing in a swing.
All the women had run away scared,
Mother and father were missing.

'Was it the sun risen in Nanda's house?
Or was it the moon hiding from eclipse?
Perhaps it was a doll of blue diamonds,
Brought to life by providence.'

Like her lost calf the cow had found,
Pootana's mind was now at peace.
The mother's eyes were filled with love,
She watched with single focus.

To kiss his soft cheeks,
She put forth her lips.
By itself dripped two streams
Of milk from her nipples.

Uncontrolled she stretched her hands,
And headed straight forward.

The god of the devotee rose,
And moved to her lured.

From her breasts, Mother Pootana
Wrung out and fed him milk.
Men and women of Gopa
Were hiding and watching awestruck.

Spreading out all his limbs,
God was suckling in slurps.
Motherly heart of Pootana
Was filled with utter joy.

She said, "My son, what for
You left me and came away.
I have gone crazy, dear,
Searching for you blindly.

"With such pain, I've birthed you,
Holding on to walls and pillar.
Searching for you frantically,
My mind had turned bizarre.

"I'll take you back to Mathura,
I've found my lost treasure.
I'll not leave you for a moment,
I'll keep watching your face like mirror."

Hearing the words of Pootana,
God stopped suckling.
He watched the mother's face,
Tears from his eyes were streaming.

The three-day-old started speaking,
"Listen, dear Mother.
Hearing your words, I am melting,
Like salt inside water.

Leaving Mathura, I came here,
To perform my play at Gopa.
It has been destined that I'll grow,
In the lap of Mother Yashoda."

Pootana said, "It's alright, my son,
If you don't want to be in my lap.
Then keep me in your lap,
As long as I am alive."

"So be it!" said the Lord,
And suckled with all his strength.
Along with milk, he sucked away
Mother Pootana's breath.

---

* *Gandharva/ Gandharvi – demi-gods and heavenly musicians.*
Gandharvi (feminine)

Juapuni*

The sun has set across the hill,
Water lilies have bloomed.
On the fence, the ridge gourd flowers,
Were smiling in mellow mood.

Pure white *kains*^ flowers,
Around the fields they stood.
Antar^ and *Shirel* flowers both,
At each other they looked.

Against dark clouds, flew by,
A flock of cranes stark white.
Middle of the village, children called,
"Cranes give, Cranes please provide."

In the cremation ground jackals howled,
Herder brought home the cattle.
At the basil plant, grandma lit a lamp,
And raised the wick a little.

The flies slept and mosquitoes arose,
Making buzzing noise.
Against the bedbugs they contested,
"Let's see, it's either you or us."

The moon arose like a basket,
The night lush with flowers of *kia*^.

The roads and banks turned bright,
Like the day, it looked clear.

Dhindak dhatur, Chindak dhatur,
*Madal*** drums began to beat.
Eleventh day ritual was over,
Today was the cooling rite.

They went around the outline squares,
As drummers played the *Dalkhai*@ tune.
Singing and gyrating their hips,
Danced a group of young maidens.

Games they played, bhasar, Kabaddi,
Marbles, *chiti, gudu, bahuchuri*.#
Busy in games, people passed the night,
Forgetting each their worry.

Girls played *Chhilo Lai, Humo*,#
The older women played dice.
Devotees got Radha and Krishna to gamble,
Krishna lost and paid the price.

Dussehra came and business stopped,
Purses were all empty.
Karni, kalasu$ rice they ate.
At times raw, at times not tasty.

Gunji, Mandia& were left to eat,
Bakes of rice bran with salt.
Income and wages were gone,
Even broth of rice was short.

In days of scarcity comes *Juapuni**,
Makes everyone very jolly.
Making us laugh and play,
It goes, leaving us lively.

No sweetmeats, no alcohol,
Neither curry of meat.
Though it is a dry fest,
It creates quite a beat.

Those who laugh and let laugh,
They are the great people.
Salutations to you, *Juapuni*,
Come well and go well.

Same people mayn't be living tomorrow,
Even about rice broth we can't be sure.
If we happen to be living,
We shall meet the coming year.

■

---

* *Juapuni* – A festival that is on the full moon following Dusshera festival (Literally means Gambling Full Moon Day). It's customary to play gambling games that day.
^ *Kains, Antar, Shirel, kia* – types of flowers
** *Madal* – A kind of drum, @ *Dalkhai* – A folk dance and folk music of western Odisha
# *Bhasar, Chiti, Gudu, Bahuchuri, Chhilo Lai, Humo* – types of games, mostly played indoors, at times accompanied with a tune.
$ *Karni, Kalsu* – Food items, & *Gunji, Mandia* – Types of grains, not much preferred.

Regard for Soil

Hirakud dam is completed, full will be the reservoir;
On Mahanadi banks all villages will soon go underwater.

Government has announced, "Your homes now abandon;
Those who don't leave now, in the water they will drown.

"Government will pay later, for your land and homestead;
With your families and belongings, without delay vacate."

With fear for their lives people in all directions fled;
In forests and hills, they lived and slept upon leaves spread.

Pitapali villagers had left, but some were still lingering;
At the village entrance, they were conferring.

Dulna, the lone, scruffy old woman, with a load on her head,
Came out of the village and was scurrying away with speed.

The path of the woman, some naughty boys obstructed.
"What items have you stolen from the houses deserted?"

Dulna said, "I have not picked up anyone's belonging;
This soil of my seven generations I could not bear leaving."

The boys said, "You ragged old woman, how do we trust you?
You're waiting for this chance, where people kept gold you knew."

"Let's see," demanded they and pulled her bundle down;
It got ripped and lumps of mud scattered on the ground.

Children burst out laughing, "Old woman has gone senile;
Take back all your wealth, on the road they are lying."

Old woman Dulna, gathered the mud, and said she crying,
"Real wealth is the soil of my birthplace that I am carrying.

Where I die, this soil should be poured on that place,
Old Dulna's soul will then rest in peace.

Bulbul

This filthy animal, the dog, I very much abhor,
Until they pooped out, I would unto them clobber.

They dare not cross my fence when I am looking,
To finish the clan of dogs, like the devil I am standing.

In drains, rubbish heaps and upon dirt what they lick,
Thinking of it I cannot eat, I feel terribly sick.

Some days ago, my son Nilu, a puppy home he brought,
He is keeping it as a pet, in my mind I am distraught.

At mealtimes he feeds it with a whole plate of food,
He dances picking it up, and pets him very good.

He goes to bed with it and showers it when he is bathing,
He has named it Bulbul and calls it with liking,

Seeing my son's deeds, I was vexed beyond control,
Out of anger I said, "Nilu have you no shame at all?

"A filthy animal, a puppy you've brought it home;
It has sullied the house by entering every room."

Nilu said, "Father a domestic animal lives at home always;
Where does it say in forests and hills it should go and stay?"

My only son, my dear Nilu, the apple of my eyes,
I could neither bear nor yell, I put up with his rubbish.

One day, at eleven, I bathed and returned from the pool;
Nilu wasn't home then, he had gone to his school.

Seeing me the puppy ran up to me, its tail wagging,
Raising its paws, at my legs it started licking.

Out of anger I burned and picked it up with my hand;
I tossed it out over the fence across the backyard.

Bulbul fell with a splash, the next house had a well;
A load was shed from my head, that was how I felt.

From school returned Nilu and Bulbul he did not find;
He searched every corner, as if he was out of his mind.

Later he got to know that I had let it drown;
He laid down in an inner room with a sad frown.

He didn't eat or drink and didn't get up and sit;
Two days he cried piteously for his dear pet.

I consoled him saying, "Nilu, why are you so staunch?
A mere puppy it was, why do you miss it so much?

"It's dead and gone, why bemoan? A new puppy,
We shall get, roaming in the streets there are many."

Nilu said, "Father if someone kills me, and instead,
From the streets gets you a new boy, will you consent?"

Animals and Humans

Deep in thoughts, I was going one afternoon,
I heard the wails of a puppy, full of mourn.

I went close and saw the road was getting tarred,
In the summer, the coal pitch was blistering hot.

A little puppy was entangled, its legs in tar were caught,
To pull it out I ran across the coal tarred road.

Said the contractor, "Don't touch, it might bite."
Hearing him I backed out and thought of its plight.

At that time from somewhere the mother ran to its child,
Biting, jerking and pulling, she freed it and placed it aside.

It seemed the dog told me, "Fie to humankind,
Human by name, but with no justice nor mind.

"In the jaws of death was my child was yelling;
For your child would you just watch standing?"

Cursing myself, I came away from that spot;
Contrast between man and animal, tormented my thought.

What Do We Do

All street dogs, one day, held a massive gathering,
Politely they called every dog, without much barking.

Down the lake was a large field, there upon they rallied,
An old dog, the wisest one, presided and took the lead.

A shaggy dog spoke first, "Quiet all of you.
A danger has befallen us; What do we do?

"People are keeping foreign dogs, Alsatian is the breed,
They care for it, lodge with it, give it a bath and feed.

"Hungry we subsist, sleep in garbage dumps, and look unkempt,
Those who see us fling sticks at us and beat us till we yelp.

"Dumping the native for the foreign is a blunder by man!
We'll soon be wiped out, if we don't work out a plan."

Another one got up and said, "Listen my fellow brethren,
These days human dung is not suitable to consume.

"Earlier days, their dung smelt of ghee and butter,
Now it stinks of fertilizers and pills, times have altered."

The president got up and said, "Brothers, quit this silly talk,
Let's discuss the main point, keep out the nonsense joke.

"The reason we are dogs is that we don't tolerate another dog,
Humans are following our nature; our value is now lowered."

What Else Could Have Happened

When old Surku into death throes came,
His son said, "Father chant Ram's name.
Chant Ram Ram, chant Ram Ram."
Surku said, "Ram Ram I'll surely chant,
But on chanting Ram's name what does happen?

"If one chants Ram's name, son, what does happen tell?
Pray explain in simple words, if you know it well."
Turned up Yama,* while old man Surku spake,
A noose and stick in hand, Surku's life to take.
Surku said, "Wait, O king Yama, you cannot take me away;
First explain what does happen on chanting Ram's name, I pray."
Yama said, "I don't know, but Lord Indra might know;
The king of heavens would have the answer, to him let's go."
Yama took Surku's life and headed for the heaven;
To Indra he said, "O King, for you here's a problem.
Upon chanting Ram's name O brother, what does happen tell?
Pray explain in simple words, if you know it well."
Indra said, "Let's go to Brahma, I don't know it myself,
He'll have the right answer, why do you trouble yourself."
Along with Surku and Yama, Indra went to Brahma's abode,
They asked him, "We have our hopes on you, tell us O Lord;
Upon chanting Ram's name O Brahma, what does happen tell?
Pray explain in simple words, if you know it well."
Brahma said, "Let's go to Shiva, I don't know it myself,

Shiva will have the right answer, why do you trouble yourself."
Indra, Brahma, Yama, the three of them carried Surku's life;
At *Kailash***, Shiv Baba's abode, in haste did they arrive.
They asked him, "Tell us Shiva, you should know for sure,
A human soul has questioned us, but we have no answer.
Upon chanting Ram's name, O Shiva, what does happen tell?
Pray explain in simple words, if you know it well."
Shiva said, "I would have told you had I known the truth,
Let's go to Vishnu and ask him, he resides in *Vaikunth*^."
To *Vaikunth* went, the human soul, Shiva, Brahma, Indra and Yama,
They asked, "Tell us Vishnu, you must solve our dilemma.
Upon chanting Ram's name, O Vishnu, what does happen tell?
Pray explain in simple words, if you know it well."
Vishnu said, "What more can come about?
Even as gods, you are unable to make out.
Ram's name chanted a soul at the time of his death;
Travelled he to heaven, to Brahma's abode, then to Kailash.
Finally he has reached ^*Vaikuth*; what else could have happened?
The query of a human soul you are unable to apprehend.
"In Ram's name is such greatness, even unknown to gods,
Bandit Ratnakar achieved liberation chanting Ram's name backwards.
Not ordinary, Ram's name is truth; it is the substance of the world;
The wise know the name liberates from the ocean of the world."

* *Yama – the god of death*
** *Kailash – the abode of Lord Shiva*
^ *Vaikunth – the abode of Lord Vishnu*

Lantern

On top is attached clear glass,
Within burns fire of violence.
Wealth is the fuel filled,
Hence it blazes more intense.

When the fire burns very strong,
The glass will crack to smithereens.
Stoking the fire of violence within,
Duryodhan landed in utter ruins.

Fire

Creation of life on Earth
Earth, water, air and ether
And Fire puts them all together
With five elements the body is born
Then it's called a lifeform

Whence it comes and where goes
Who it is, it knows not
In falsehood it proliferates
Limitless its desires and lusts
When it sees, it covets

Thousands of lamps are alight
Oil wicks can be counted
But fire is only one
Fire of Param Atman burns in every soul
Stand aside, and see it all

Too Much

Too much salt makes the taste go bad
Too good a sorcerer is devoured by god
Too much money danger brings
Too much devotion is the trait of thieves

Too much beauty shows lack of manners
Too much discrimination is lack of morals
Too talkative is the fraudster's trait
Too simple is considered dim-witted

Too charitable a man begs and borrows
Too much of rains and the field overflows
Too clever it is, look at the crow
Mornings it eats the garbage we throw

Too much sweetmeat attracts pest
Too faithful is a poisonous trait

■

Profit

First some seeds, sows the peasant,
And takes care of the paddy plant.
After harvest, he does reckon,
A small start but a good return.

With initial amount of a few scores,
Goes the tradesman for commerce.
After negotiations, give and take,
Considerable profit he does make.

In deep forest the sage sits upright,
Without food he does meditate.
Devotion is his prime investment,
God will be his future reward.

Starts the poet to pen a poem,
He sees some and misses some.
Literate people when they read,
Their appreciation is his benefit.

Profit and loss is the game of life,
The game ends when time is ripe.
The profits that people look for,
The giver fulfils their mind's desire.

Kamdhenu*

More and more I am in need,
Above my topknot a tassel I need.
Through my mind, fly wishes like wind,
A house eighteen stories I wish I build.

Servants at my beck and call,
Wealth spilling out through rear wall.
People would call me the overlord,
They would follow me at my word.

Choicest of foods I would eat,
Greatest of people I would meet.
Jewellery on me would not lack,
A stash of cash in my backpack.

Knee high bed and pillows soft,
I would lie and snore in comfort;
Many a young and pretty maid
Would contend to be my bride.

*Jeen*** bird chirped, "Stop, beware,
"Strongly bind your fence barrier.
Kamdhenu is a cow of craving,
It robs its owner's peace of mind."

---

* Kamdhenu – A cow in mythology that fulfils every wish of its owner. Here it implies the endless desire that resides in man in the form of a milch cow
** Jeen – a type of bird that is believed to chirp aloud when someone is about to die

Greatness

With matted hair, wearing tree-bark,
the Baba shuffled along the lane,
Through a village path he trudged,
Biren Brahmachari was his name.
A woman was irritated seeing the Baba's stance and comport,
She hurled abusive words at him, like a blow they did hurt.
"Die and lie in a ditch you lazy man; to avoid fending
for your family,
You are keeping away from work; look at how you
pretend to be holy.
Such thick arms, your fat body, meant for crows and dogs to eat,
Dependent on others, you glutton, fie on the life you lead."
Smiling slightly said the Baba, "*Alekh Swamy Akeh**."
The woman said, "Loads you can gorge, begging in the
name of Alekh."
Despite the scornful words Baba wasn't in the least angered,
He took it that she knew not, or else she would be well mannered.

Those who wear dark glasses, to them black the world appears,
The thief sees everyone as thief; to the saint all are virtuous.
Had it been any other Baba, he would have cast on her a curse,
The clear-minded Biren Baba could not be touched by sinful words.
Hundred times greater is the one who tolerates than the one who censures,
One who considers past and future, listens quietly and endures.

∎

---

* *Alekh Swamy Akeh – Alekh is the name of god indescribable; Baba utters the name here as a religious incantation.*

The Jealous Always Suffer

In digits the biggest is Nine, its pride is the highest,
Smallest is number One, but it stands on the crest.
To the numbers said Nine, "Let's not keep One on top;
Headbutt it from the bottom, let it get thrown off."
Nine bumped Eight, Eight bumped Seven,
Seven bumped Six, Six bumped Five,
Five bumped Four, Four bumped Three,
Three bumped Two, Two bumped One.
Against whom does One collide? Only zero on other side.
Unto Zero it said, "Brother, they butt me with their head.
I'll fall down and spill, a way out of it, please tell."
Zero said, "One, listen. I'll stand to your right.
Let's get down together, don't you at all bother.
As I go on increasing, your value will go on rising."
They got down and became Ten. All digits were in a spin.
The jealous always suffer. In the end they're the loser.

Make No Silly Excuses

The sun was setting smiling,
Into the lap of Mother Nature.
A pair of doves was flying by,
They settled on a tree branch.

Winds of July came swooping low,
Pebbles and mud started to roll.
Trees bent down with the swoosh of winds;
A storm was gathering full.

The pair of birds started to worry,
They had left their chicks behind.
They might fall and die somewhere,
Or get blown by the stormy wind.

"You arrogant stubborn wind,
What benefit do you draw?
What mistake did we commit,
That you've made us your foe?

"How many chicks you've killed?
Made us cry with your pride.
When all of us you have killed,
Only then will your anger subside!"

On the tip a palm tree leaf,
From its nest spoke a sparrow,
"So easily you blame the wind,
You are yourself so shallow.

"According to season come wind and rains,
According to season summer and winter.
You merely think of filling your stomach,
But for good of the world is the weather.

"Like us sensibly plan,
And make yourself a nest.
Wind, rains, cold or dew,
Without fear you can rest."

---

* *The title selected by the poet (Chali na jani batara dosha) is an idiom in the vernacular, which literally means 'If you don't know how to walk, blame it on the road'. Instead of a literal translation, the translator has used its meaning – 'Make no Silly Excuses' – as the title.*

Summer

It's April end, Summer has started,
Heat of the sun is beating down.
Rivers and streams are bone dry,
Grasses and plants are wilting brown.

Earth is parched by the hot sun,
The loo winds are howling.
With it the jungle has caught fire,
It's best to speak not a thing.

Sweat dries to salt on the body,
Prickly heat pokes fun at you.
One is tortured by unease,
Helplessness is killing too.

Out of thirst, the throat is parched,
Ears and nostrils start burning.
When will the dastardly Summer go?
People wish rains to start pouring.

"Rains and sun come in equal measure,"
Thus spoke the men of yore.
"Bear the pain, then comes the gain,
Keep this in mind, children dear."

Rains

At sunset the fireflies flit,
They spread out everywhere.
Dark clouds start closing in,
From the Northwest corner.

Whooshing sweeps in the wind,
Swirling dust all around.
Rolling down the roof's edge,
Pours down water in torrents.

Clouds roar in thunder,
In flashes strikes lightning.
In the fields and village roads,
Streams run down gurgling.

Insect's scream and cricket's chirp,
Everywhere it is shrilling noise.
The frog welcomes the rain,
Ululating in cheerful voice.

Generous men save a part,
Of their hard-earned money.
Like the rains they donate,
To benefit others liberally.

The Harlot of Tikarpada

She was about twenty-five, her name Madhavi Parida;
I asked, wherefrom she hailed, she replied, Kendrapada.
I said, "Sister why do you do such immoral trade?
Womanhood you are tainting, your dharma you've betrayed.
Earn and eat, you'll get enough food, wealth is only fleeting,
Merely for wealth you have turned a woman for the keeping.
Man is keeper of wealth, but knowledge is the keeper of man;
Being lazy to work, you have defiled your body, O woman!
It is in the Indian culture to remain one man's wife,
By your immoral work you are beyond societal life."

Hearing my words said Madhavi, "Listen awhile brother,
These days no one cares for the bride's beauty and calibre.
All over India, the scourge of dowry has spread,
For dowry brides are killed, in papers have you not read?
Jewellery, TV, scooter, sofa set, if parents have supplied,
They accept the bride though she may be lame or one-eyed.
We are poor, we cannot give jewellery, scooter or car;
For lack of dowry, I am at my parents', unmarried so far.
The money I earn now by selling my body, I shall spend,
To buy heaps of dowry, when I go as a bride newlywed.

■

The woman hails from Kendrapada, but she conducts her trade in Tikarpada (hence the title)

Danseuse

To the beat of the olden drum,
Started to dance the danseuse,
In the scorching midday sun,
Perspired her body profuse.

Smooth and dark, slim her waist,
Clothes were sparkly with laces.
Twirling around raising her garb,
She struck curvaceous poses.

Bracelet, armlet, bangles on her hands,
Silver-like gleamed but were false.
Earrings, nose-pins, studs,
Nose-rings, hoops all made of brass.

In her curly hair, the parting
Was held down with hairclips.
Her tasselled hair in a shiny knot,
Held in place by jingling stickpins.

In *Sampur* tune sang her man,
In harmony to his drumbeat,
"Gazing at the beautiful clouds,
Go, O cloud and tell my mate…"

Crowds of onlookers came in rush,
They stood around in a circle close.
In women's group a whisper rose,
They raised eyebrows and a nose.

One said, "Fie, O fie,
Shameless is this adulteress.
She's cast away all shame,
This loose in morals temptress.

"What prestige and status has she?
A dancing woman, a streetwalker.
Shows herself to tempt young men
A thousand men she does lure."

An old woman crossly spoke up,
When she heard such natter.
"Neither streetwalker nor temptress,
The danseuse is Sati Sita.

"When Ram was exiled to forest,
Sita too turned a forest dweller.
Husband drums the wife dances,
How's the danseuse in error?

"She is happy to serve her husband,
Spends her days under the trees.
Like parrot and mynah they fly around,
That's nothing but heavenly bliss."

■

Demon

There lived a demon king in *Satya** Yuga,
With pride he flew his flag of ego.
Having won Shiva's boon, he spread terror;
His name – Hiranyaksh – had letters four.**
 'I, Me' was his constant boast,
The demon bragged always 'I, Me, Myself'.
But did he not bite the dust?

When *Treta** Yuga arrived,
Fourteen worlds he occupied.
His name Ravan** – one letter less;
He showed off his brute prowess.
'I, Me' was his constant boast,
The demon bragged always 'I, Me, Myself'.
But did he not bite the dust?

The three worlds, he threatened,
When he stomped, the earth trembled.
To letters two his name was curtailed;
In *Dwapara** Yuga, Kamsa** he was called.
'I, Me' was his constant boast,
The demon bragged always 'I, Me, Myself'.
But did he not bite the dust?

Of wealth and status one who is proud,
They think they're the best in the crowd.
For them a letter is further restrained,
They always say 'I' with proud disdain.
'I, Me' those who do constantly boast,
In this *Kali** Yuga, they are the demons;
For sure, they will bite the dust.

---

* *Satya Yuga* – *According to Hindu Scriptures, there are four Yugas or ages – Satya, Treta, Dwapara and Kali.*
** *four letters* – *The word 'Hiranyaksh' has four letters in the Sambalpuri-Kosali language. Similarly, Ravan has three letters and Kamsa two letters in the vernacular.*

On the Death of Budhadev Das Cries Mother Samlei

Where have you gone away, Budh, leaving me behind,
You've not died, son, rather you've throttled Samlei.

Hope I had on you, son, that you'll uphold my honour,
My dearest, in your youth, untimely you passed away.

Having you, I was so delighted, my dear son,
Making me childless, you left, my pride is gone.

For you your mother will cry, you thought not once,
Holding my hands and legs, I am sunk in remorse.

I was blind in the darkness, you showed me the way,
People were all praise seeing the Karamsani play.

Thinking of your good deeds, cries your brother Haldhar;
Never did you let him go, how could you distance yourself, Dear?

I've lost you, my precious jewel, my pride is broken,
Calls Samlei, Budh, Come back to my lap again.

Kunjel Para

Samblapur town reverberated, O!
Ghumri Drum started beating.
Mounted on an elephant,
Came Veer Surendra, the king.

Accompanied by sons and subjects,
Village headmen and zamindars,
As though the king of Gods in heaven,
Lord Indra was journeying outdoors.

At their doorsteps, women and girls,
Were watching merrily.
Setting water pots and lighting oil lamps,
They were ululating shrilly.

Dancing and prancing people celebrated,
Waving their hands and sticks.
"Victory to Samlei, victory Samlei,"
In unanimity they shrieked.

Liquor, hash or opium it had had,
The elephant went out of control.
Stampeding, trampling, crushing,
It made all sorts of turmoil.

Whoever it saw, it grabbed with its trunk.
And trampled them underfoot.
Breaking the throng, helter-skelter,
In panic people did scoot.

It charged ahead and charged back,
Like a young bull in rage.
Tearing fences and thatches, people ran;
Some on branches, some on treetop stage.

The mahout fell down flat,
His chest was ruptured.
The king was sitting like a pillar,
The elephant was speeding forward.

Much commotion and wailing,
Defiled seemed the village.
Offerings with water were pledged,
Mother Samlei, keep us safe.

Riding a horse, was following
The zamindar of village Ghens.
His name Kunjel, caste Binjhal,
Of sixty bulls was his strength.

He rushed and grabbed the elephant,
Like in a tiger's clutch.
Roaring like Bheem, he struck with goad,
The elephant could not budge.

Like arum cooked in tomato curry,
The elephant was without strength.

It trumpeted and fell down,
The king got away unscathed.

The king ran up and held the arms,
And embraced Kunjel Singh.
"Good you came and saved my grace,
My boat was about to sink.

"You are my right hand, Kunjel;
You are my brother divine.
To you indebted forever,
Is King Surendra Sai.

"Sambalpur with you I share,
This side of Mahanadi river.
Let it be known from today,
That it is named Kunjel Para"

Ghumri – a type of drum

First Clean Yourself

Wealth he has immeasurable, but gives to no one even a trifle;
Involved in fraud and bribery, his name is Dharamkari.
He has accumulated like a miserly saver;
'If I save enough,' he thinks,
I'll be able to live forever.'

A holy man of *Mahima** faith, Baba Birendra,
he wore garbs of leaf;
On his head were locks matted,
a palm umbrella his left hand held.
He was passing by that street;
Dharamkari came and laid himself down,
At Baba's feet prostrate.

He said, "O Baba mercy me, from dangers many save me;
Age is no longer on my side, many ailments have got me tied.
There isn't a moment of delight;
O Sire consecrate me in the *Mahima** faith,
So that I may live in bliss without fright."

Baba said, "For that you need to give and let give,
do and let do;
The whole day I have been fasting,
to find some food I was hoping.
Give me some alms before we get started;

Let me eat and my body revive,
Only then can you get consecrated."

Dharamkari was full of delight,
to get some food he went inside;
Fries, vegetables, *dal, badi***,
a plate heaped with rice and curry;
With these fare he returned quickly;
From somewhere an earthen bowl,
Found Baba and picked up swiftly.

He sat cross-legged on soil, and said, "Serve me in this bowl."
Cow dung was in the pot, and also in it was a wiping cloth.
Dharamkari to Baba told,
"Out of a bowl soiled with cow-dung,
How will you eat food?"

Said Baba with a slight smile, "I am amazed at your words;
Like this bowl dung defiled, similar is your living style.
First your own self, you need to clean;
Your unclean body should I consecrate,
For you and me both, it would be great sin."

■

---

* Mahima faith – A religious faith / teaching which dictates a religious lifestyle.
** dal, badi – different types of food or dishes

The Younger Brother's Courage

The eldest daughter-in-law was in labour, tossing turning,
Unable to deliver, out of anguish she was screaming.

Medicines, quacks, witch doctors, had been of no gain,
From morn till evening, she had been writhing in pain.

In Patnagarh, the shadow of doom caused much concern,
Any moment her life might end, the queen may be gone.

Shakti arrow struck Lakshman, Ram with his monkey army cried,
The same way, with sons and subjects, King Narsingh cried.

An old man said, "There's a way, but time is scarce,
Rice is into the husking log, telling now is no use.

"Going and coming is tough, dark and stormy this night,
With rain waters, River Mayavati should be in spite.

"But for that, I know for sure, in village Barpadar,
Lives a lowborn named Sudurni, she can surely deliver."

As soon as Babu Balram Dev heard this from the old man,
He started off from Patnagarh without waiting an instant.

Raining it was in torrents, with lightning and thunder,
Whither path, whither river bank, all had gone under.

Fields and yards were submerged in overflowing waters,
But went on Balram, with no hesitation, no fears.

To reach Barpadar, River Mayavati he swam across,
Carrying Sudurni on his back, he returned on the rush.

Like monkey on crocodile's back, the midwife sat on Balram,
River Mayavati filled to the brim, right across, he swam.

Soaking wet, he entered home, the midwife on his shoulders,
The queen was relieved when the midwife got her to deliver.

Happily saw the king, a boy was born,
Praised he, "O brother, you're the talented Lakshman.

"Of eighteen forts you are supreme, O King of Hirakhand;
If you ask, I'll gift you my kingdom and quit Patnagarh."

"If you wish, brother just give me the jungle across River Ang
Balram likes to hunt, we'll go there for shooting big game."

Throughout the kingdom, people said, "Hurray, hurray."
The Younger Brother's Courage! A fact that's like a story.

Why Did He Leave His Home

The minister's visit was on schedule,
The village lanes were packed to full.
Since a month it's been proclaimed,
Those that have any complaint,
Before the minister should narrate.
Whether or not anything be done,
Folks struggled with hopes elevated.

They hoped a proper road to be constructed,
Steps down the riverbank would be concreted.
Over the temple and the clubhouse,
Thatched roofs would be taken down,
And concrete roofs would be built instead.
All jobless youth roaming about,
Would be able to earn their daily bread.

Bore wells would be dug in village ground,
The pond would be embanked all round.
If the minister they could please,
Food and clothing would come with ease.
The government would pour in funds,
The contractors and their men,
Hoped to usurp sizeable chunks.

Over the stage was a colourful canopy made,
On the table a flowery sheet they spread.
On that sheet was placed water in a glass,
Next to that were flowers kept in a vase.
And on the sides were rows of seats;
To receive him with garlands they went,
To the accompaniment of drumbeats.

Bananas ripe, bunches of grapes,
Baskets full of juicy mangoes,
Were laid out for the minister's treat,
Rasogollas* and many other sweets.
Plates were full of such fare
All these were a bait to get a good catch
Of this everyone was well aware

Our villager, Phagnu the blind,
By begging he made a living.
Been without sight from birth,
He was groping and rushing forth,
To the minister to narrate his woes.
If he could block the minister's car,
He would be relieved of his sorrows.

Speeding came the minister's car,
Phagnu fell with his face downward.
He was crushed under the wheel,
The pain of dying he didn't feel.
People said "Good that he met his doom.
He knew the minister was coming;
Why then did he leave his home?"

On everyone's lips there was this talk.
Triumph is never for the poor folk;
Water always downward flows,
Fault to the deprived always goes.
People said "Good that he met his doom.
He knew the minister was coming;
Why then did he leave his home?"

---

* *rasogollas – a tasty and popular sweet*

Warning

We have our government, we no longer need,
foreign agriculture,
Soil of India has turned to rubble, all animal life is dying, O!
Quit foreign methods, despite our eyes,
blind they've made us.
Quit foreign methods, with sweet potatoes they've duped us,
Quit foreign methods.

Talking of high yield plans, whole country they've churned,
Chemicals and pesticides have polluted water, air and soil, O!
Down with illness and diseases, death beckons at half the age;
Down with illness and diseases, one day we'll all be hollow,
Down with illness and diseases.

Fertilizers, pesticides and seeds are being sold by
foreign companies,
They are enjoying sweet jaggery,
all wealth they've sucked away, O!
The noose is round the farmer's neck,
all twelve months, he feels the ache;
The noose is round the farmer's neck,
finally dependent he comes to beg,
The noose is round the farmer's neck.

The farmer who fed a lakh of mouths, where can he be found?
He is struggling in debt, yet for another loan he begs, O!
Look at his sorry plight, taller the bamboo hollower inside;
Look at his sorry plight, the farmer is merely a brinjal dried,
Look at his sorry plight.

Discard chemicals and hybrid rice,
farm with cow-dung manure,
*Jhuli, Sunakathi, Magura, Sampri, Karni Tulsibas,** O!
Let there be a clean India, let the foreigners go their way;
Let there be a clean India, then shall our value stay,
Let there be a clean India.

---

* *Jhuli, Sunakathi, Magura, Sampri, Karni Tulsibas* – types of homegrown paddy

Swachh Bharat#

The sky, land, water and air, dirt-free environs,
India is going to be a clean and developed nation.

Away from village, dig a pit and dump your garbage therein;
Roads, banks, lanes, drains and sewers, keep always clean.

Close to villages, trees and stumps, felling be forbidden;
Who does not know, O brother, trees give us oxygen?

In fields, ponds, on roadside, to relieve, do we need?
Toilets in every home government will provide.

Foreign art and culture is making us fragile,
If we wish, we can set right, now is the while.

One East India has quit, but 5000 have come in;
Fumes from factories rise, the air is now unclean.

Smelly fertilizers and pesticides are used in farming;
Animals that benefitted humans are nowhere to be seen.

Potatoes, brinjals, tomatoes and other vegetables,
Though good-looking, are filled with toxic chemicals.

Wherefrom came polythene, all items are packed in it;
Biodegradable they are not, burning is also a threat.

People are quitting villages and heading to the town;
Polluted air they breathe and live all the year round.

Towns are mines of flies and insects, creating many a disease;
Ramdev Baba says yoga and *pranayam** people must practise.

New diseases daily appear, doctors aren't aware;
Rushing are doctors too to the hospital of Vellore.

Jhuli, Sunakathi, China, Magura, Sampri,^ let us cultivate,
Crops grown with cow-dung manure will be there to trade.

Discard chemicals, hybrid rice, they're foreign material;
Let's turn back, a clean India, that's what is essential.

Hindus, Christians and Muslims, we are all Indians;
Ram, Krishna, Allah, Muhammed, Jesus, all are one.

Since many Yugas, united is India, cannot be divided;
In Swachh Bharat, brothers, let the Tricolour be hoisted.

∎

\# *Swachh Bharat − Clean India campaign,*
* *Pranayam − a breathing technique in Yoga*
^ *Jhuli, Sunakathi, China, Magura, Sampri − varieties of indigenous paddy*

Mahua Tree

Listen to the merits of mahua tree, in mind the merits do bear,
Its wood makes firewood and leaves make plates
and bowls; O hear.

Twice we reap its fruits, mahua and its dried seeds,
The sap of mahua sprout relieves the body of aches,
Oil of mahua seed apply, the skin gets smooth of cracks;
O hear.

With an axe or sickle, if wounded is the body,
Peel the fruit and fill the wound with its fluid,
Fester it won't with water, in days four you'll be cured;
O hear.

If your tooth is shaking, brush with the mahua twig,
The sin of killing a cow, under the mahua is absolved,
For weddings, seven seats set, the mahua is made the witness.

We give it the position of god; O hear,
The tree is a true god; O hear.

Butterfly

Fluttering flies the butterfly, from hither to thither,
Drinking nectar, it flits from one flower to another.

Two pretty wings, in a variety of colours painted,
To catch it and place it on my chest, I'm tempted.

It was once a caterpillar, its body poisonous,
Bristly and hairy all over, its sight obnoxious.

By and by it changed its fearsome attire,
It's turned a butterfly that people admire.

Moving from ignorance to wisdom, one's life does alter,
Knowledge and education are the wings for man to soar.

From darkness to light, from hell to heaven, let's move forward,
Like the butterfly, life will progress, and we'll be honoured.

■

Neem Tree

O dear neem leaves   Who recognises your qualities
O dear neem leaves!

In March dark purple   Leaves start to sprout
Add to sour dishes, the neem flower seeds sizzled in hot oil
Or cook with greens,   it mixes and goes well
O dear neem leaves!

The bane of itches and skin ailments, grind and take for stomach upset
For toothaches rinse the mouth with neem water at the right time
The bark if one boils and drinks, diabetes goes away.
O dear neem leaves!

Neem oil is used on wounds, flies and insects to keep at bay
Dried neem fruits and leaves make the right manure for fields.
Mentioned in "Manoranjan Shalimar", the verses let us recall.
O dear neem leaves!

Smeared with Colours, The Old Man was Cremated

With the approach of March, eager were children,
To play with colours on *Holi*.*
From upper lane to lower, they met with such jolly.

From each lane, for fifteen days they've been collecting donations,
High is their excitement.
Some stole, and some pestered their mothers for the payment.

The fest will dazzle this year, chicken feast in the night,
To drummers they've paid advance.
When the band plays, it'll be fun to sing and dance!

Palsa# flower with banana juice, the stain does not wash off,
Keep your water guns ready.
Relations no bar on festivals, we'll smear on everybody.

Keep aside a pant and shirt, at that time you might forget,
Powders of many a hue.
Buying will be managed by the well-informed Raghu.

That morning, the chowkidar announced time and again,
"The old zamindar is dead.
All residents come out now with your shovel and spade.

"The village is unsanctified, non-vegetarian food is debarred,
For three days, O brother.
Stop the play of colours, stop eating prasad;
worship is also banned."

The joy of children came to end, colours in pots they had made,
They were disappointed and said,
"That damned old zamindar, had to wait so long only to die today!"

Chamru, Sukru, Manglu, Ghan, their anger was beyond mention,
They came up with a pretence.
On the body of the old zamindar, all pots of colour they dispensed.

Smeared with colours, the old man was cremated, his life was a success;
Such a life is meaningful.
Anyway, colours meant for entire village was used up by a single.

---

* Holi – Festival of colours, people smear colours on one another
# Palsa – A bright red flower that has no fragrance

Radhe-Krishna

Radha Krishna's many-hued acts,
Around Vibhu have been characterised.
But the main role played by the queen,
The poet colourfully paints here.

Through scriptures and books,
I am heading close to Radha.
O merciful, of your benevolence,
A sprinkle I wish to receive.

The prime man, Parameshwar,
Is God Shri Krishna.
Show me that way by which,
You could attain Him,

Tolerating insult, blame,
Danger, risk and hurdles,
Crazy with anxious mind,
Radha remained faithful.

The path which you travelled,
Paramatma you could acquire.
Kindly show me that path,
That much is this poet's desire.
*

Completing his act in Gopa,
Kunjvihari Kanhei to Dwarka went,
Eighteen days of the great war,
Mahabharata came to an end.

Thinking of Radha's love,
Hari was getting restless,
His state of mind, to anyone,
He was unable to express.

People see hot flames,
If the forest is ablaze,
But if the mind is afire, who sees?
The person burns within.

Krishna's disquiet mind
Was seen by the populace,
A yagna for peace they decided
To conduct in Dwarka palace.

The disquiet Krishna would sit
In the yagna as the Karta,
Sage Narad went to the three worlds,
Invitations to distribute.

He chanted Hari's name, smeared with sandalwood paste
And basil garland around the neck.
Saffron clad, a veena in one hand,
In the other castanets, he held.

Riding on his mind-craft,
All fourteen realms, he was roaming.

The mischief-maker, Narad sage,
Through the skies, he was travelling.

Vrindavan came on the way,
Sitting was Radha sitting on Yamuna's bank.
She was gazing to the right,
Her palm on the left cheek.

Her eyes were wet with tears,
Both cheeks had sunk inwards.
Seen was her bony waist through
Clothes tattered and unwashed.

The hair on her head was matted,
Nearby lay her earthen pot.
Seeing her, Narad with compassion,
Descended to Vrindavan.

Not a sound of birds to hear,
Crickets chirped everywhere.
Yamuna river was bone dry,
Not a creeper for a bird to hide.

Kadamb tree was withered,
Branches fell crackling down.
Animals were nowhere seen,
Of thirst and hunger, they were scrawny.

Even in March, hot winds blew,
The heat of the sun was unbearable.
Upon Vrindavan was it the time of doom?
Branches and leaves were in gloom.

Without Krishna, wealth and matter
Of Gopa were without splendour.
Where the distraught Raee sat,
Presented himself Narad there.

When Radha saw Narad's face,
She bowed to ground many a time.
Brimming with tears were Narad's eyes,
God as witness, he bore in mind.

'All twelve months in Vrindavan,
Mango-scented breeze had blown.
Flow of Yamuna that never ended,
Now its basin was bone dry.

'Flowers bloomed and spread fragrance;
Birds of all kinds tweeted sweet.
Rasleela^ they played under the Kadamb,
With flowers and fruits the trees were laden.

'Radha who enchanted the world,
Dearer than life for Kanhu she was.
Now crazed, possessed, unkempt head,
Drained, shattered, she looked fully aged.

'Great O Fate, great you are,
In dust you fling, a heavenly flower.'
To test her mind, in clever guise,
Spoke Narad in delicate voice.

"Raee Vinodini, how is it that
You've wasted your golden self?

Enchanting figure you've discarded,
You look lost and out of mind.

"Who made your appearance such?
No smile, no joy on your face."
Said Radha, "O great sage,
What matter to you is secret?

"That same Radha I am still,
But missing is Kanhu's love.
Radha's affection he tossed aside,
To Dwarka went Kala-Kanhei.

"For whom do I dress up well,
He has left me and gone away.
His merits I am recalling now,
Hanging myself should I die?

"In dreams, I see him but not in sight,
but when I wake, no respite.
If I die, I would ever sleep,
Then forever, I could get his sight.

"The body of earth will mingle in earth,
Staying alive why do I suffer?
In all limbs and blood of Radha,
To the brim, Hari is filled.

"If I hang myself, within me,
I'd kill Kanhu and a sinner be.
Killing a cow is death destined,
Attack by cow too is death destined.

"Tell, O sage what must I do,
Which way must I take to die?
Queen Satyabhama, Jambavati, Rukmini,
Must be eighteen times better than me.

"Adorned pretty with eight jewels,
They must be charming Kanhu's mind.
Golden cot with pillow and bed,
Perfumes must be amply spread.

"Naphtha, myrrh, sandalwood paste,
They must be applying on Kanhu's limbs.
Special betel in his mouth they offer,
Each queen is prettier than the other.

"In the bond of love, they have tied him,
Cowherdess Radha is dying of despair.
I'll dress in flowers for whose sake,
Like *jhalmali** I'll die of shame.

"Even so, Narad, he would forget me,
That's something I don't believe
Like the first morsel is always tasty,
First love always remains alive.

"First, Duti as a mediator,
Hari had sent her over.
Hitting, scolding I sent her back,
He came himself after that.

"I chased him out with rude words,
Angered by it did he punish me?

Once he went to Chandra,
That time I got him to despair.

"Sitting aside throwing a tantrum,
How often I have shown him temper!
Using words hurtful, I have scolded,
Now I am repenting over it.

"Grudging did Kanhu disown me?
Made me wipe tears with my sari.
Though he has distanced me,
From me, never separate is he.

"New playful, actor Hari,
Life of the living, Kunjvihari.
Peacock feathered jaunty quiff,
Wreathed in beads, the apple of my eyes.

"Tinkle-tinkle his anklets chime,
Armlet, and bangle his arms adorn.
Under the Kadamb, he stands cross-legged,
That's where Radha's life is tied.

"O sage, I have hopes on you,
Take me close to Kanhu.
To heart's content, I'll see him once;
Reflecting on him, I'll stay home then.

"Seeing the untidy form of Radha,
Kanhu will disdain raising his nose.
Alas! I better not go very close,
From a distance, I'll see his face."

Narad said, "Listen O Raee,
From Dwarka, I have come running.
Tomorrow Hari will conduct a Yagna,
He has sent all me to invite.

"Hearing of invitation to Gopa,
Chief Queen Rukmini disagreed.
Even so tomorrow, a few gopals,
with king, queen and Madhu Mangal,

"Will be going uninvited,
Though from Gopa none is wanted,
Go with them, O Radha;
See Kanhei and your anguish ease."

Radha's heart was full of pleasure,
As though she found a lost treasure.
Narad departed in his mind-craft,
At Yamuna, Radha sat and watched.

Full night, the cowherds of Gopa,
A wink they didn't sleep a wink.
Readying their bags and bundles,
Pacing they were up and down.

With the morning star rising,
Eagerly they called each other.
The happiness of the cowherds
Was endless to speak in words.

Cheese, rabdi, milk and curd,
They carried in pots many.

With King, Queen, and distraught Radha,
From Gopa they departed.

Amongst them, they talked and laughed,
As they walked the route.
"Seeing us, he'll rush up to us,
Oh! the dark Kanhu Vanmali."

Someone said, "I'll feed him cheese,
Taking him in my lap."
Another said, "I'll rock him,
Holding him on my hip."

Radha said, "You all stay behind,
And let me to the front.
To get a glimpse, I have come,
With so much love and hope.

At Dwarka's Lion Gate,
Arrived the residents of Gopa.
There at the gate, holding a spear,
Was standing the guard upright.

Radha said, "O Guard,
Would you please let us in?
People of Gopa, we've come,
To meet our Krishna Kanhei."

Said the guard, "Residents of Gopa,
Have you got an invitation?"
Shaking her head, replied Radha,
"No, we have received none."

The guard said, "Chief Queen
Rukmini's orders are stern.
Gopa residents if they come,
Out they should be thrown."

Cowherds said, "Ours is Krishna,
Where's the need for an invitation?
Without being told, we can come,
What for do you question?"

Said Radha, "O guard,
Go and tell Krishna Kanhei,
Nanda King and Queen, Gopa's cowherds,
And with them has come Raee."

In the inner chamber, Rukmini got to know,
The cowherdess had come.
Furious she charged up to them,
Like the cobra of the doom.

She shouted, "Where's she, that Radha?
Who's that street roamer?
She had held my Lord, in her bind,
With some bewitchery."

Radha said, "O Chief of Queen,
I am that Radha.
To see my Kanhei, I have come,
Running up to Dwarka."

Grinding her teeth, growled the queen,
"O, you are his Gopa mate!

You have learnt all the charms,
Today you'll get back with interest.

"You are the flotsam of Gopa,
Unwanted you move through the woods.
My Lord is the king of Dwarka;
You've got his mind crazed.

"Whole night he startles,
'Radha, Radha,' he mumbles.
To Vrindavan you ran at night,
Immoral, shameless, loose character.

"Clever Duti was your go-between,
From you to him, she set the link.
Cowherdesses have no prestige,
Villages they roam selling curd.

"Your time is over today,
In slices your skin will pare.
Co-wife's jealousy is banana stain,
The karma's fate you'll bear."

Said Radha, "O Chief Queen,
How do I explain to you?
Get me beaten and killed,
But let me for once see Kanhu."

Rukmini said, "You'll see, wait.
Why are you so impatient?

"Guard, take the horsewhip
And beat her nice and proper.
Kanhei romance, Kanhei longing,
All her craze will disappear."

On the queen's order, the guard
Hit her with the horsewhip.
Like a prawn she twitched about,
Flailing rolling on the ground.

Pitiably she wailed, "Save, O Kanhei,
Save this Radha's life.
Before my life goes, Kanhu,
Just once show me your sight.

"Radha's body that couldn't bear
The weight of jasmine flowers,
Today her body is gashed,
With whiplashes all over.

"From many a danger, you had saved
the people of Gopa, O Benupani.
With you there, in your knowledge,
Radha is being disgraced.

Giver of love, O Radha-Madhav,
Show yourself now once.
Seeing your face, this Radha's life,
Let it end rather forlorn."

At the yagna, as the Karta,
Was sitting the God Hari.

Hearing Radha's desperate cries,
He could no longer endure.

Lashes rained on his body,
The beatings of the horsewhip.
Nose, ears, body, and head
Got slit open and bled.

Shaking and shivering,
Quickly stood up Damodar.
Seeing him said Balram,
"Kanhu, wait awhile more.

"Yagna rituals aren't yet over,
Where are you getting up to go?
If unfinished, it will be a fault,
We will later have to repent."

Said Krishna, "Look, Brother,
Whiplashes on my body.
How do I bear any more?
Slit and bleeding are my wounds."

Balram said, "O you Kanhei,
You are such a pretender.
Who beat you, and how is it,
We could not see the offender?"

"Come and see, Brother,"
Said Krishna and went running out.
At the Lion Gate, the Chief Queen
Got the doorway shut.

Rukmini saw the Lord's body
Was dripping with blood.
Chakradhar was crying
In sniffles his tears flowed.

Rukmini said, "Tell O Lord,
who put you in this state?
In fourteen worlds, which gutter-sleeper
Has got the horns on his head?"

"You got me into this state,
O Rukmini, who do I blame?
Superficially, you are devoted,
But got your husband beaten."

Surprised said Rukmini,
"Are you blabbering in your sleep?
Being your wife, at your feet I serve,
why my husband should I beat?"

"If sunlight appears dark,
Then Rukmini herself is blind,
In jealousy, ego, pride, fame,
Wealth, and status you're tied.

"Radha Krishna's Ranga incarnation
Is one tree with two branches;
Two nostrils but a single nose;
Of one river we are two streams.

"Radha and Krishna are not different;
Broken they cannot be apart,

Throughout life, their souls
With love are attached.

"This body filled with flowers and fruits
Is Vrindavan, which has no compare.
Radha Krishna's twin figure,
Therein they roam together.

"You too think, Chief Queen,
That Krishna is your husband,
Only with my shadow you play;
From me, you are distant.

"Jealousy, ego, pride, fame,
Wealth and status, those who desire,
Despite all worship and rituals,
With them I stay not a while.

Give me way, O Rukmini,
I am getting desperate."
Opening the door, went out Hari,
Pushing Rukmini aside.

With whiplashes from the guard,
Spread out Vinodini was lying.
"Kanhei, give me your glimpse,"
Was all she was saying.

In front of the half-dead Radha,
Krishna presented himself.
Said he, "Radha, awake and see,
I am Kanhei, the mountain-lifter.

"Come, Radha, into my arms,
My life is in despair.
When your body mingles in mine,
I will feel at peace."

Swiftly got up Radha and saw,
'Who is this holding a discus?
With yellow silk and eight jewels,
His body is bedecked.

'Shining on the head is a crown,
In dress and stance, a warrior.'
Startled in surprise said Radhika,
"Who you are, I know not."

Krishna said, "O Radha,
Am I not your Krishna?
Radha's Krishna, Krishna's Radha,
A single limb are the two of us."

"My Krishna's features are missing;
You are not of Radha.
Royal jewellery was never seen
On Radha's Krishna.

"Radha's Krishna is multi-styled,
Forest flowers he donned.
Eight jewels were never
On his body adorned.

"Beads of trees he wore,
And a peacock feather in his hair.

In triple loincloth, crossing his feet,
He danced under the Kadamb.

"Playing the flute, minds he charmed,
Casting a sidelong glance.
I had come here rushing
To find that Kanhu, perchance.

"This Krishna I don't need,
You may return to your home.
I will return to my Gopa-pur,
Wiping my fate of karma."

As she stepped back to return,
Mayadhar cast an illusion.
In Krishna Kanhei's triple-curvy pose,
He stood as the new Natvar.

Jaunty quiff and curly hair,
In it a shining peacock feather.
Strings of abrus beads he wore,
With it garlands of forest flowers.

On his wrists silver bangles,
On his arms armlets jingled.
Triple loincloth around his waist,
And on his hip a silver waistband.

Anklets tinkled on his crossed feet,
And he held the Mohan flute.
As he played it, Radha's body,
On its own enlivened and shook.

Just as a magnet pulls iron,
He drew Radha to him.
Dwarka it was or Vrindavan,
Radha could not discern.

As the cobra raises its hood,
And sways to the Naga tune,
Similarly, Radha in a single mind,
Came running in a straight line.

Hugging Krishna Kanhei,
She leaned on his chest,
Her heart and life merged in him
Like lightning merges in the clouds.

In the brightness of the rising sun,
Like the morning star dissolves,
Like the river joins the ocean,
And is no longer visible.

Slowly from Krishna's chest,
She slid downward,
Upon his crossed legs, Raee placed her head
and departed.

Krishna picked her up,
Radha was no more.

Let us all Radhe-Krishna, Radhe-Krishna, meditate,
In this illusive world, there is nothing else left.

■

^ *Rasleela* – *dance of divine love*
* *Jhalmali* – *a flower that has no fragrance.*

The Matter Ends Here

From abroad returned home, Swami Vivekananda;
O, what a joy once he touched the soil of India!

With esteem his countrymen stood ready to felicitate;
With gratitude he was filled seeing the people crowded.

Utterly beautiful, young and attractive there was a maiden,
She was trailing Swami-ji, not losing him for a moment.

Finding a timely break, she approached him politely.
"Swami-ji, my entreaty do keep," she spoke frankly.

"Let's make love once in a secret affair;
By you to bear a son, that is my desire"

Said Swami-ji, "Dear Mother, save me this occasion;
To birth a boy, time is needed, yet it may not happen.

"Your son I am from today, and you are my mother,
Bonded we are as mother and son, so bother me no further."

He walked ahead another twenty steps or so;
Countless people were crowding in the flow.

India's triumph slogans rented the atmosphere;
A few college students stood in the front there.

One of them asked, "Swami-ji, India you applaud;
Why then do you wear shoes made abroad?"

Swami-ji said, "Dear friend, what make is my turban?"
The boy said, "Who doesn't know? Turban is Indian."

"Know this, boys, Mother India on my head I bear.
Foreign lands I revere, yet their goods on foot I wear."

The Minister and the Beggar

At the minister's house turned up
A beggar begging for food.
Minister said, "Get lost you fool,
Begging is not good.

According to your capability,
If you work for some stranger;
You'll surely get paid,
You will not die of hunger.

To eat free you beg at each house,
Why do you disgrace yourself?
Do not lose your prestige,
As long as you have life."

The Beggar said, "O Minister,
More than you is my prestige;
Working on the sly, the nation's wealth,
Say, do you not seize?

People all over curse you by name,
Your seventeen generations they efface.
More than me you lack honour,
Your parents are a disgrace.

For hunger in my belly I beg,
But selfish I am not;
Self-centred you are, better start begging,
Like me from house to hut.

God Kalia of Priest Luru

Fat and paunchy Luru, the priest,
Drumming his chest, he danced.
His wooden idol of Kalia,
He adored impassioned.

Where there is love, there is value,
Love is utterly sweet.
If there is love, Lanka is nigh,
Or else, it is far outside.

Pleased the zamindar of Toshgaon,
Gave Luru the wooden deity.
On its head was a silver crown,
Four to five ounces* it was weighty.

He could well be the younger form
Of Indradyumna, the king.
Luru's greatness he recognised,
And gifted him a great thing.

Everyone called him Luru;
Shankar, he had been christened.
Born into the *ganda*^ caste,
In Ghess, the valiant land.

Who knows perhaps Dasia Bauri
Had been reborn as Luru.
At his call, Lord Jagannath,
Came out of the Puri temple.

On a brass plate he carried his Kalia,
And roamed the villages for alms.
Whatever he received from people,
He offered Kalia first, and ate only then.

When he slept, next to him,
He placed Kalia to sleep.
Lurus's Kalia, Kalia's Luru,
Hearts of each other they keep.

From Phuljhar, Luru was returning,
When it got evening midway.
The night he passed under a tree,
At a shrine beside the roadway.

With the cock's crow, he awoke,
To bathe early in the morn.
He found Kalia was missing,
All thoughts from Luru was gone.

Calling out to Kalia, cried Luru,
Agonising, beating his breast
"I never left you for an instant,
You left me in this state!"

Without food and water, he slept,
Under that tree face down.

In his dream Kalia spoke,
"Hey Luru, I'm in the dung mound."

He got up and Eastward,
He ran in haste disordered.
Like the cow that has lost her calf,
Moos and runs wayward.

Stinking garbage, full of flies,
Repulsive to the nose,
In a man-high ditch of dung,
Kalia was lying supine pose.

Luru said, "In this manure heap,
You lie in tantrum, dear.
Where you threw your silver crown?
Your head is looking bare.

"Let's go, while it is still dewy,
We have to walk a long way.
How much fruits you want to eat?
At Sohela it's market day.

"Were you testing me:
What will Luru do?
Your silver crown did they snatch,
The thieves who took you?

"Let them take the crown away,
Don't be gloomy of heart.
Until Priest Luru is alive,
What can be your dearth?

"Extending my arms, I call you,
Kalia, come running to my lap."
Rushed up Kalia, the Lord,
And sat on Luru's hip.

■

---

* *Ounce – The original poems uses 12 – 15 bhari, which is converted to equivalent ounces in this translation*
^ *Ganda – a low caste*

Bhai Jiuntia#

Of Jarasandha's scare Krishna Balram hid in a termite hill,
Doom struck in Dwarka town, people and children in peril.

Revati* to the eight chief queens^ in their ears told,
Take your children and escape to your mothers' fold.

To save their esteem all married ladies,
Fled to their mother's home territories.

Beautiful Satiya, of the land of Koshala, to Krishna was married,
She too fled, but with her, Krishna's sister Subhadra she carried.

The family was fearful and scattered, disaster was on the brink,
The younger sister was worried most, she couldn't sleep a wink.

On the eight day of Dushera, a fasting ceremony
Subhadra performed,
With faith she observed the rite so that her brothers may
not be harmed.

In nine colours she wrote God's names in a maze of
sixteen block(s),
She bathed and cleaned herself waking up at the crow
of the cock.

Coconut, sweet rice, vermillion and grass-stalk she offered the deity,
Oil lamp and incense she lit and prayed for her brothers' safety.

With folded hands she laid prostrate and begged for help,
"I shall serve you forever if my brothers return safe."

Pleased the gods and goddesses gave a boon to Subhadra,
"Your brothers will live until the end of *Dwapara*.**

They will not drown in water, burn in fire nor be slain by the sword,
Your brothers are in one piece, right behind you, just turn around,

Subhadra turned back and saw Krishna, Balram standing,
With gratitude to their wrists she tied the ritual string.

From then on, in the land of Koshala, Bhai Jiuntia fast they observe,
Brothers and sisters wish well for each other, tied in a bond of love.

---

* *Revati – Balram's wife*
Balram – Krishna's elder brother
Subhadra – Krishna's sister
^ *Eight Chief Queens – Krishna's wives. Krishna had 1600 wives, of them eight were Chief Queens. (One of the Chief Queens – Satiya – was from Kosala.*
# *Bhai Jiuntia – a festival in western Odisha where sisters fast and pray for long life of their brothers*
** *Dwapara – One of the Yugas. There are four Yugas, viz: Satya, Treta, Dwapar and Kali*

Spring Tune

Blooms *Palsa* flower, and wafts the scent of mango blossoms
Mahua fruits drop from their bunches ...
To the rhythm of gentle breeze, O friend.
The cuckoo sings in the branches
The cuckoo sings in the branches

Flutter the red new leaves, O dear.
O, the new leaves ...
From one flower to other roams the black bee
O, the black bee ...
In forests and jungles, in ditches and trenches, O friend
Sprinkles of colour everywhere
To the rhythm of gentle breeze, O friend
The cuckoo sings in the branches
The cuckoo sings in the branches

Vying with each other bloomed *Girel* and cotton, O dear
O, *Girel* and cotton ...
Golden bunches of *Sunari* flowers, look at their passion
O, look at their passion ...
The *kurey* flower smiles at the tip of the branch

The lover will kiss its cheek
To the rhythm of gentle breeze, O friend.
The cuckoo sings in the branches
The cuckoo sings in the branches

Toordhinda, dhinda, dhinda, the Mridang starts beating
O, the *Mridang*^ starts beating ...
Tinkle, tinkle, chime the lassie's anklets
O, The lassie's anklets ...
Lavanya's curly hair is tied, O friend
In a bun with strings of jasmine
To the rhythm of gentle breeze, O friend.
The cuckoo sings in the branches
The cuckoo sings in the branches

We bow in reverence, Goddess of the Jungle
At your feet we bow, O Mother
At your feet we bow ...
Fifty-six crore lifeforms you feed, Goddess
You feed, O Goddess ...
Well-wisher you are at all times, O Goddess of the Jungle
We worship you with a *Karam** branch
To the rhythm of gentle breeze, O friend.
The cuckoo sings in the branches
The cuckoo sings in the branches

■

Palsa, Girel, Sunari, Kurey – *types of flowers or flowering plants*
^ *Mridang* – *a type of musical drum*
* *Karam* – *a branch kept aside as a worship ritual*

The Morning of March

Boom, boom bangs down,
The rice husking log.
Cock-a-doodle-doo,
Starts crowing the cock.

Creak, creak, creaking,
Went the water lifting crane.
Rumbling sound makes the loom,
In the weavers' lane.

Coo, coo, coos the cuckoo,
Birds chirp among the trees.
In gusts soft and cold,
Blows the spring breeze.

Rat-a-tat-tat, Rat-a-tat-tat,
The knocking bells on oxen.
Scrunching goes the bullock cart,
On the uneven rocky turn.

Ding dong, ding dong,
Ring the temple cymbals.
Fragrance of jasmine spreads,
While its pouch the bee fills.

Ghutur ghut, ghutur ghut,
Coos the pigeon bird.

Surr, Surr milking sound,
Makes Surghutu, the cowherd.

In full brightness,
Rises the morning star.
Malati's mother mops the floor,
With cow dung at the door.

A man with nasal sound coughs
While he hums 'Kanhu Keshab' song.
In the morning sings the oilman,
Who lives down the palm zone.

Early morning unto Ghaesaan,
Calls out Khatkuri.
They go to pick mahua fruits,
With baskets in a hurry.

Cook-coo sings the cuckoo,
The wife of the season Spring.
Hidden in mango branches,
She plays hide and seek.

Slowly rises the sun,
Red colour is its peak.
Fluttering fly swans in flocks,
And settle on the lake.

Sparrows chirp and trill,
On the roof thatch.
Caw, caw, the crows caw,
In the morning of March.

A Song in Sanchar Tune

In the wind and water of this land my life is made
In the wind and water of this land
Green and beautiful forests, O what nice hills
Flowing down are many streams
In the wind and water of this land

The glory and greatness of this land, flutters the flag of this land
This land gives us golden harvest, this land gives us grains
The fragrance of this land is sweet, O what a sweet smile
Listen to the cuckoo singing
In the wind and water of this land

Of this land are valiant Surendra Sai and warriors Madho and Hatey
One was banished, another jailed and another sent to the gallows
The poets of this land Bhima Bhoi, Gangadhar, and Khageshwar
Oh what they wrote
In the wind and water of this land

The truth in this land, Goalti Rath, Hari Shankar, Narsingh Nath
O Mother Goddess Samlei, with devotion I join my hands
Be it Sambalpuri, or be it Kosali, it is sweet like jaggery
How great is this language
In the wind and water of this land.

The Soul is Real

It was a dark new moon night in the palace of Mithila,
King Janak was sleeping next to Queen Sunayana.

He saw a dream: A foreign ruler has conquered Mithila,
The borders are surrounded by foreign militia.

The subjects of Mithila are now under their order,
They are screaming, "Kill, behead, go get Janak here!"

Out of fear the king is running away by the outskirts,
"Kill him," they are screaming and chasing him with swords.

Across the pond in a jackal's den, he hides hushed like a prey,
At a quiet time, he comes out and runs to get away.

Ahead he finds the seven seas; there is no way to flee,
'What to do!' wonders the king and tries to break free.

He looks behind to find a cobra chasing him to bite,
A tiger from the front is charging with jaws open wide.

Thinks Janak, 'I cannot carry on with my life any longer,
Snake and tiger have surrounded me, soon they'll devour.'

Just then the snake strikes and on the leg there's a wound,
Gushes blood from the gash and flows on the ground.

Roaring the tiger pounces on him and one arm it bites,
"O father I am dying," he cries out; his eyes shut he writhes

He opens his eyes to find the snake and tiger both gone,
Bent forward, crying in pain the king starts to run.

Ahead he comes across a desert, no trees or no shade,
In the afternoon the sand is hot, in the sun's blazing raid.

Up to the knees his legs are scalded, his feet full of blister(s),
His stomach growls; he is famished out of thirst and hunger.

'What will I eat, how will I survive?' he starts to ponder,
'No trees, nor leaves, no creepers nor plants, nothing over yonder.'

At a distance he sees a man holding something in a bowl,
To the poor and hungry he was offering food as dole.

Out of hunger, runs the king there, his own life to spare,
He sees a stable-cleaner handing down the fare.

He thinks, 'Yuck, food from a low caste, how do I partake?
But if I don't eat this very instant, my life is at stake.

Let my caste get defiled, but my life should not end.'
Joining his palms he seeks alms, like a starving vagrant.

Seeing his face the stable-cleaner recognises the king,
He says, "O king, food from a cleaner would you be accepting?"

The king says, "Look brother give me some food right away,
Why discriminate while dying, my life is not likely to stay."

Looking at the bowl the cleaner taps his forehead and says,
"O King, all food that was cooked I have already given away.

The food left at the bottom, Let me scrap out and offer,
I'll cook again and serve, eat this for now to endure."

All the leftovers from the bowls the cleaner does gather,
From above he pours into the king's palms joined together.

At the rear, some bulls are fighting, shoving and jostling,
The king falls down on his face, the bulls go over him trampling.
*

Distressed, the king screamed aloud, "O I am dying, I am dying."
Queen Sunayana startled awake and wondered what was happening.

Chest pounding the king sat up, hard was his breathing,
The queen said, "What happened, O king, how are you feeling?"

The king said, "Just a while ago I was a mere beggar,
Now I see, I am king with wealth, subjects and stature.

Was that real or is this the reality, have you knowledge any?
Can you explain the matter to me, O Sunayana Maharani?"

The queen said, "To your question I have no answer,
Let's find the answer by calling pundits from all over.

Beating the drum, a guard announced all over the kingdom,
He who gives the right answer shall get half the kingdom.

In Mithila pundits gathered from every direction,
To win half the kingdom was their main attraction.

The pundit from the west said, "The dream is unreal."
The pundit from the east said, "The dream is real."

The pundit from the north said, "Both are unreal."
The pundit from the south said, "Both are real."

The king said, "Your answers are neither proper nor exact,
Without knowing the truth, shots you cast in the dark."

To their homes returned the pundits from four directions,
Reflecting upon the dream the king remained anxious.

One day a sage named Yagnabalka arrived in surprise,
The king received him with esteem knowing he was wise.

The sage said, "O saintly king, are you hale and hearty?
I can make out that within, you have some anxiety."

The king replied, "O great sage, on this night of last week,
I saw a dream: A foreign enemy to my kingdom laid siege.

'Kill, kill' they shouted, with weapons drawn they chased me,
Out of fear I escaped and ran up to the shores of the sea.

A snake bit me and a tiger too, I was famished and tired,
The sand was scorching en-route, my feet got all blistered.

Out of hunger I ate from the hands of a lowborn,
In a bull-attack my body and limbs were torn.

Without help I cried in sorrow and in disgrace,
When I awoke I was cosy in my royal palace.

The dream or this awakened state, which is the reality?
O sage, not knowing the truth, I am full of anxiety."

Smiling the sage said, "O king pay attention and listen,
You felt it real until the dream was in your vision.

But when you awoke the vision turned unreal,
Similarly, this illusory world appears to you real.

When you die this waking state will also turn unreal,
That is unreal, this also is unreal; only the soul is real."

The Slaying of Kalapahad*
(An episode from the poem Shri Samlei)

Resounded the *Dulduli** drums,
And played the *bharni*^ melody.
Before Mother Samlei, Balram
Poured water in entreaty.

Sweaty it was in the sanctum,
With smokes of incense and myrrh.
Vermilion, kohl, garlands of *Dahana* #,
And red hibiscus flower.

Burned the lamp with seven wicks,
Fistfuls of white rice were put.
Squatted the king with folded hands,
And prayed with eyes shut.

"Keep us safe, O Mother Samlei,
Upon us has come a danger.
Sambalpur I'll have to leave,
And go away without honour.

"Like the doom, charging ahead,
Comes the devil Kalapahad.
I cannot fight against him,
He'll crush my bones hard.

"From Bengal he has brought,
Selected fighting forces.
Due to him all kings of Odisha,
Are living in distress.

"Three deities of Puri Temple,
He burnt down to ashes.
For their lives, the priests and servitors,
Fled to distant places.

"Gajapati Raja Mukund Deva,
He beheaded and put to death.
Hindu temples he destroyed,
And Gods he buried in earth.

"Now has come your turn Mother,
You have to keep your flag aloft.
Take the form of furious Kali,
And their heads you chop off.

"Pitching tents, they've camped,
At Shankar pond across.
Sambalpur in the morn,
He will invade with his force."

Before Balram finished talking,
A possessed *barua*[1] arose in fury.
Into his body had entered,
Mother Samlei Maheshwari.

Gnashing his teeth in anger,
He seethed looking furious.

He said, "O King, do you think
Kalapahad can return to his place?

"He doesn't know who I am,
He'll know, wait just a spell.
Taking six of my sisters along,
With his blood I'll play hell.

"Does he think a weakling
I am, like Ramchandi?
Pretending to get water,
I'll slip away into hiding?

"He got away on the East,
His ego is now stout.
I'll pierce him with the trident,
His innards will spill out.

"Committing sins over and over,
His burden is now enough.
He has come to face me now,
The mother's brood I will snuff.

"Why should he come here?
I'll go out to him ahead.
You'll see, waking in the morn,
Kalapahad's body dead."

Reverberated conches and bells,
The possessed man fell flat.
Each to their home returned,
And the temple door was shut.

The sounds of the night played,
On the lonely village route.
Gusting the southerly winds
Were swirling dust about.

Chirping cheeping everywhere
Swooshing sounds were heard,
Whooshing was the burning fire
Swishing and hissing aloud.

The *Dumbroo*[2] started beating
And bells began to ring.
Bells on waistband went jangling,
And necklace pieces tinkling.

"Wait for me, come, let's go,"
They were calling aloud.
Chiming went the ankle-bells
Bangles jingling, they walked out.

Near Shankar pond had camped,
The forces of Bengal.
Three scores of tents were pitched,
Packed with soldiers all.

Seven young women entered therein,
Gorgeous, fresh and pretty.
Lustily the men were drooling,
When they looked at their beauty.

One girl carried curd and milk,
Another sweets and pancakes.

Someone took puffed rice,
One other fried chickpeas.

Some took custard apple, bananas,
Someone lime, tangerine and orange.
The girls could at most be,
About twenty-two in age.

Cajoling them here and there,
They offered coaxing each.
"On final day, you may pay,
Eat until you are pleased."

The entire troops of Bengal,
The girls fed every soldier.
Happily, they gobbled a lot,
Till they could eat no further.

Soon after they dined,
Black diarrhoea they suffered.
Wherever each was lying,
On that spot they died.

At last was left the lead man;
He was alert out of fright.
"Wherefrom came these seven girls,
To me at dead of the night?

"Without taking any payment,
They offered food and enticed.
They had some hidden motive,
No one could ever perceive."

He came out and saw his troops,
Everybody was lifeless.
Those lasses had deceived,
And done them all to corpses.

Kalapahad was full of fright,
He darted to get away.
The seven sisters chased him,
Their fearful forms in display.

Clanging were their bells on waist,
Tongues they stuck out hanging.
Hair let loose, they looked scary,
Cleavers and pots they were holding.

Blood-curdling cries they screamed,
And surrounded Kalapahad.
The demon shrivelled out of fright,
He dropped down prostrate.

Chandrahasini and Metakani,
Over his two legs stood.
Sureswari and Ghanteswari,
Crushed his hands underfoot.

On his head trampled
Goddess Patna-Pataneswari
On his crotch stood straddling
Goddess Bhawani-Manikeswari

Goddess Mahakali-Samlei,
Into his chest pierced the trident.

Kalapahad's game of raids,
Then and there came to an end.

Victory to Goddess Narayani,
Victory O Samlei Goddess.
Ages after ages, for the world,
You incarnate in readiness.

In the ten days of *Dusshera*
You take ten godly forms
Tara, Mahakali, Sodashi, Matangi
Bhairavi, Dhumabati

Dhabla, Bagla, Bhubaneswari,
On ninth day Khendia Mundi,
Mother Maheshwari, in March
You take mango, mahua offerings.

To the hopeful and faithful,
You always stand by their side.
For believers you're God, to sceptics mere stone,
O, You are Goddess Shri Samlei.

---

* *Dulduli – a kind of drum, famous in Western Odisha,*
^ *Bharni – a tune,* # *Dahana – leaves of a tree named Dahana*
1. *Barua – A man possessed by god or goddess. When possessed, what he speaks is believed to be spoken by the god.*
2. *Dumbroo – A small hand-held drum*
**Kalapahad was a general in the army of Bengal Sultanate in the mid-sixteenth century. He was intent on attacking Odisha, plundering the temples, and desecrating them.*

Conscience

Beans, cucumber, bitter and sweet gourds,
And fruits in bunches sprouted.
Okra, brinjal, tomatoes and chillies,
Were getting into baskets packed.

I got greedy and thought of stealing,
I could make some quick money.
I would then afford a knotted bracelet,
And wearing it I would look shiny.

I slipped out that dark night,
Crickets were chirping loud.
I cast a glance in all directions,
There was not a soul around.

Carrying baskets I reached the farm,
I braced myself with my gear.
Eyes darting, chest pounding,
I reached out shaking with fear.

All of a sudden, within me,
Someone said 'Stop there!
With a noose, *Yama** will pull you
Your sins he will not spare.'

From the side if the owner sees you,
He will pound you with a baton.
You will taken before the headman,
Your prestige will be trodden.

Sweating in the sun he has worked,
Hauling an eighteen-foot water-lift.
If you steal as much as on a needlepoint,
You will lose by a winnowing-fan full.

From greed comes sin, from sin death;
Give up greed, cast it aside!
Never can sin be covered or hidden,
Lie is black and truth is white.

I returned home but didn't get sleep,
Dawn came about slowly.
And then in a while,
The red sun rose up brightly.

An octogenarian, a ripe old man,
I met him on the village road.
Into the old man's ear I spoke,
Plainly the night's episode.

Said the old man, "In the worldly trap,
Man is caught struggling with greed.
The conscience knows the way out,
It speaks only if one pays heed."

---

* *Yama - God of death*

Just Think of It

Whether you steal and rob or help others,
You tell lies or the truth,
Just think of it:
Omnipresent God is watching you.

Whether you eat cheese cake or rice-bran bake,
You drink milk or broth of boiled-rice,
Just think of it:
Once inside, it's all the same sludge.

Whether you are good-looking or ugly,
You sleep on a bed or on the floor,
Just think of it:
In the end insects will swarm the body.

Whether you are rich or a hungry pauper,
You are a family person or singleton,
Just think of it:
You have come alone and will go alone.

A Letter to Poet Haldhar

Here's a letter to you O Haldhar!
Even like going through pains of labour,
Creative poetry you should deliver.
Here's a letter to you O Haldhar!

If you want to clean the society
First cleanse your own self
If you wish to pull someone higher
First climb a couple of steps
Seeing the attractions of the world
Don't let greed put you to bother
Here's a letter to you O Haldhar!

The greatest of all creations – humankind
Is now groping in darkness
They are harassing others no end
For their own happiness
Dharma, karma and shame renounced
 They are heading to hell further
Here's a letter to you O Haldhar!

Consider sorrow as happiness
A blessing is Mother's reproach
Where there is poison there is also nectar
Passionately go and search

Take poison yourself but distribute nectar
If needed, carry on your head Ganga river
Here's a letter to you O Haldhar!

Make everyone in society your own
By speaking words sweet
Make the whole world a single home
In that family you inhabit
Use your pen with all your might
The society to set in order
Here's a letter to you O Haldhar!

Light of the Earthen Lamp

When the earthen lamp is lit,
It lights the inner chambers;
Like upon seeing the moonlight,
Out of fear darkness scampers.

Like in the darkness of ignorance,
The bandit Ratnakar roamed;
Upon seeing the light of knowledge,
Into Sage Valmiki he transformed.

Like in an heirless clan,
The lamp is lit by the newborn;
Let the wick burn and spread,
The language of Odisha- Western.

Chhanda Charan Avtar

(The thoughts of the artist Chhanda Charan Acharya before he gave up his life)

Moonlit night like *Kia* flower white,
Clouds looked like fish scales piled.
Starkly white, on a tamarind tree,
Sat a pair of cranes, he and she.

Brightly bloomed the *Kadamb* flower^,
Spreading its fragrance everywhere.
The mind Yamuna broke the edges,
Waves flooded over the verges.

Vrindavan was lit up bright,
The breeze wafted across mild.
Transverse flute I started to play,
Radha could no longer quietly stay.

To the tune of flute, she came running,
In the string of love, she had me bound.
Where the heart is attached,
There the jasmine scent is found.

The play in Gopa has ended,
The *Kadamb* tree has wilted.
The mind Yamuna is parched,
Into bits the flute is smashed.

Radha is gone, but her love is around;
Where on earth shall she be found?
Radha has gone to the other world;
At my crossed feet her life she laid.

I am coming, Radha, for me await,
Upon this earth I will no longer stay.
You are the mynah, I am the parrot;
To other side of clouds, let's fly out.

Creeper swing has started to beckon,
I shall swing in it dangling down.
The Avatar of *Chhanda Charan*.
From today comes to conclusion.

---

^ *Kadamb flower – Bur Flower*
* *Chhanda Charan – A name for Lord Krishna. It literally means cross-legged pose. Lord Krishna is often portrayed standing in such a pose holding a flute to his lips. In this poem the name of the main character is Chhanda Charan*

The Village Chowkidar

In a red turban with a pointed stick,
He is the village chowkidar.
He calls out at midnight,
"Be alert, all residents."

In cold and dew, rain and storm,
In the still darkness of night,
From lane to lane he's on the beat,
Afraid of no one he is.
With him around, thieves and robbers,
Can never cross the line.

The baby near its mother,
Peacefully lies in slumber.
It startles and babbles,
And hides under her belly.
When it does pester stubborn,
Mother calls out, "Come now, chowkidar."

Rough is his body, strong and sturdy,
Of caste he is untouchable.
To avoid touching others,
He stands aside far.
Outside the village in Dalit lane,
He puts up in that corner.

At year end ready for his treat,
He goes from street to street.
Bundles of boiled sweets, pancakes,
Fried sweet dishes and vegetable bakes,
And one anna each family gives;
He celebrates the *Puspuni** festival.

He considers the whole village,
Its people and belongings his own.
The damage and losses of the village,
He feels he is responsible.
Oldman Gandhi had set the statute,
To serve the village is to serve the nation.

∎

---

* *Puspuni* – *A festival on the full moon night of January (approx.)*

The Poet

Shri Haldhar Nag was born on 31 March 1950, in a village in Bargarh district of Odisha. Hailing from a modest background, Haldhar Nag did not receive a formal education. He did many odd jobs, in his childhood for a living. His different jobs include performing on and off in theatre groups and other village troupes, where he gave expression to his artistic talents. He took up work as a cook in a school hostel, and later set up a small cabin-shop selling stationery for students in the vicinity of that school.

During his association with schools, he started writing folk songs in his mother tongue, Kosali (the language is also known as Sambalpuri-Kosali). His writings were appreciated, and soon he recognized his own talent and started writing more poems. The first poem he wrote, and which was published in 1990, in a local magazine, was *Dhado Bargachh* (*The Old Banyan Tree*). He then sent out another four poems to that magazine, and all got published. Nag soon gained considerable fame for writing poetry with social themes.

Since then, there has been no stopping him. He has written several hundreds of poems of which he has not kept a count. Some of his poetic works include long narratives like *Mahasati Urmila, Bachhar, Achhia, Tara Mandodari,* each between 200 to 300 stanzas in length; the longest one exceeds 1300 verses. His poems carry a message for the people, and he covers themes like oppression, social issues, nature, religion, mythology.

He remembers all his poems by heart and sings them out to gatherings and crowds from his mind like a minstrel. Thus, his popularity grew as a bard.

He was recognized formally as 'Lok Kabi Ratna' by Prayog Anushthan in 1997 in a ceremony held in his honor. He received the Sahitya Akademy Award in 2014. He was awarded Padma Shri for literature in 2016. He was also bestowed with the LifeTime Achievement Award by LIC Gateway Literary Festival Organization in 2017. The latest feather in his cap is the Bhasha Samman by Kendra Sahitya Akademy in January 2019. The same year, a doctorate was conferred on him by Sambalpur University.

The poetry of Haldhar Nag has become the subject for theses by seven students of whom two have earned their PhD in literature. His poems have been translated into several languages. Prominent among these is the collection of English translations compiled as *Kavyanjali Vol-1 to Kavyanjali Vol 4*. Besides, his poems have also appeared in Hindi, Nepali, Bengali, Kannada and Tamil languages.

The Translator

Surendra Nath is a 62-year old retired naval officer, who was struck by the desire to write from his school days but could only realize the dream at the age of 54. He retired from the Indian Navy in 2000 and took up a job in an international school in Dubai. There, Surendra Nath realized writing was his second calling and wrote many short stories and articles that were published in a few magazines. After a seven-year stint in Dubai, when he returned to India, he was already fifty. He joined KIIT International School as its Administrative Officer. It was here, he took to serious writing, quite late in life.

In 2012, he pioneered and organized a National Level Children's Literary Festival in KIIT, Bhubaneswar with the participation of school students from across the country. The festival continues to be popular and is into its eighth year now. In these literary festivals, he came in close association with renowned authors like Mr. Ruskin Bond, Mr. Manoj Das and Mr. Chandrahas Choudhury, all of whom were great inspirations for him.

He chose to quit office-going jobs and settle down to writing in 2016. He has written two books - Karna's Alter Ego and its sequel, Kavach of Surya. Going by the titles, they might appear mythological in genre, but they are not precisely so. They are stories set in the present-day with parallels drawn from the Mahabharata. Karna of Mahabharata somehow turns up in the 21st century to play a central character in these novels.

One day, he chanced upon a social media post that had gone viral, about a person clad in dhoti and vest, barefoot, receiving the Padma Shri award from the President of India. He got curious about this man and started following his works. Surendra understood that language was a barrier between Haldhar Nag's rich literature and the rest of the world. He decided to translate HN's poetry into English so that a wider audience may get to read it.

Thus, was born Kavyanjali Vol. 1 in October 2016. Most of HN's works are lying with the poet unpublished. Surendra is working on a self-conceived project called Project Kavyanjali with the aim of translating all the works of Padma Shri Haldhar Nag into English and publishing them. So far, he has published four volumes of Kavyanjali.

www.ingramcontent.com/pod-product-compliance
Lightning Source LLC
Chambersburg PA
CBHW031114080526
44587CB00011B/970